MIDWEST
Foraging

MIDWEST
Foraging

115 wild and flavorful edibles from burdock to wild peach

LISA M. ROSE

TIMBER PRESS
Portland, Oregon

Frontispiece: Crabapples grow in abundance on trees across the Midwest.
They are perfect for pies, cider-making, and snacking.

The Haseltine Building
133 S.W. Second Avenue, Suite 450
Portland, Oregon 97204-3527
timberpress.com

Printed in China
Text and cover design by Benjamin Shaykin

Library of Congress Cataloging-in-Publication Data

Rose, Lisa M., author.
    Midwest foraging: 115 wild and flavorful edibles from burdock to wild
peach/Lisa M. Rose.—First edition.
        pages cm
    Includes bibliographical references and index.
    ISBN 978-1-60469-531-1
    1. Wild plants, Edible—Middle West—Identification. I. Title.
    QK98.5.U6R67 2015
    581.6'320977—dc23   2014042915

*To my Dad, for teaching me
to listen to the earth.*

Contents

Cultivating a Sense of Place

As a child, I lived only minutes from Lake Michigan. The open fields, woods, sandy dunes, and Big Lake were my playground.

I remember growing up in my mother's garden: Tall stalks of corn, overgrown zucchini bushes, large heads of cabbages—all part of the bounty grown for our dinner table. My mother canned and made preserves from our seasonal garden, but we also had wild foods as part of our harvests. The wild grapes lining the backyard fence were turned into jellies and canned juice. Morel mushrooms in the spring were added to eggs and pasta. Apples were picked off the wild apple trees near our elementary school. Wild foods were a part of my childhood.

I also remember the evening I made my first summer fruit pie. It was a hot and sweaty June summer evening in my college apartment in Grand Haven, Michigan. I made a delicious (but somewhat runny) mulberry pie, with berries I gathered alone on a sandy trail beachside. While the pie may not have been perfect, that memory of picking the berries on the trail and baking the mulberry pie in my hot kitchen remains vivid in my mind.

My culinary abilities grew, and I found myself looking to the trees, hedges, and weeds for my teas and meals at my table. Dandelions, violets, nettles, burdock, and even garlic mustard became commonplace in my recipes, and today wild foods are part of my everyday kitchen life.

As a forager, I have learned to sense and anticipate the subtle changes in the seasons, almost like a sixth sense. On sunny February days that are cold but bright, I can actually hear the sap in the maple trees begin to run. April rainstorms and warmer weather means it's time to go mushroom hunting. On muggy days in June with frequent pop-up thundershowers, I always check on the roses and elderflowers—one round of summer thunderstorms could decimate the delicate blooms that I so love to dry for tea. And nuts falling in the green gulch next to my kitchen window? I try to harvest those walnuts before the squirrels do. I feel empowered with this ability to "read" the wild world around me. I will

On an early spring foraging jaunt in the dunes and woodlands near my home in western Michigan.

My children have grown up learning about using wild plants for food and herbal medicines. Teaching children how to forage not only offers them valuable skills, but it instills in them a sense of wonder about the natural world. Here, my daughter, Emma, gathers ox-eye daisy for tea.

always have the ability to find food and these skills connect me to the natural world in a deep way.

So many of us are seeking a connection to the land and to each other. Foraging, local foods, and community gardening connect us in a deeper way to the world around us. That need for escape into the wild is very real: we desire space and clarity. I believe this is one reason foraging is gaining in popularity.

We are also making the connection between healthy soil, healthy foods, and healthy people. The food on our plate has—or should have—roots in the earth. Our industrialized food system is a root-less, industrial production model, leaving us with over-processed, nutrient-less choices at the grocery store. People are starting to invest in healthful, local, and organic whole foods for health insurance.

Wild foods are more nutrient dense. They are a source for unprocessed minerals, an alternative to commercial supplements. Wild and foraged foods could be a solution to our food sensitivities. More and more research on bioregional, traditional diets suggests gut-healing powers rest with eating wild foods that grow in our own bioregion.

Even in the city, wild foods are everywhere. Here, nettles grow in a cultivated flowerbed of roses in downtown Detroit.

Once you find those sweet harvesting spots to pick fresh nettles in the cool, spring air, you most certainly won't want to return to the eating pallid lettuce and spinach leaves sitting ensconced in plastic on the grocery store shelves. You will find yourself craving the bitter flavors of the wild chicory and will cherish finding the smaller but more flavor-packed wild strawberries you discover in the open fields of early summer.

Returning to wild ways is a refreshing shift in our community's way of life, and it delights me that this movement continues to gain momentum. For health, economy, environment, and justice, it's now quite popular for folks to trade in their Kentucky bluegrass lawn for gardens and edible landscaping, including wild weeds like burdock, dandelions, violets, and sorrel. Even if you are a city-dweller, wild foods are everywhere: dandelions in the park, basswood flowers on the trees lining the streets, nettles growing in the rose garden beds.

Paying attention to wild plants helps connect you to the land itself. Eating foods from the wild will bind you to a place: its rivers, animals, smells, sights, and sounds. Ingesting bits of the land make the place literally a part of you. You can gather the wild and bring it into your kitchen to prepare meals for friends

A delicious harvest of wild apples ready to be made into pie and applesauce.

and family, nourishing our bodies with nutrient-dense foods and our minds as we take time to connect with each other.

The end goal of foraging actually isn't gathering delicious wild edibles for a meal to grace your table, although it is certainly a great benefit. By adding wild edibles to the table, we start to value the wildness in our city neighborhoods and make space for the wild in our yards, gardens, play areas, parks, and open spaces.

For me, those moments of noticing are among the most satisfying parts of foraging, when we take time to connect to what's around us and gain that feeling of belonging and relationship. My senses are awakened. Outside I feel alive. Wild.

My deepest wish is for you to experience this, too, and to fall in love with the wild ones.

Introduction: Foraging Basics

With this guide in hand, you are ready to learn firsthand that the goal of foraging isn't only about gathering delicious wild edibles for a meal to grace the table: it's about the journey. It is the sense of peace that comes from taking time to connect to place. It's the feeling of belonging and relationship with the land. It is the adventure that can be had by everyone—no plane ticket necessary. You just have to get outside and see where the adventure takes you.

Pull, eat, repeat: an invasive species like garlic mustard is a wonderful early spring staple in the forager's kitchen—it makes a delicious and utilitarian pesto. We can help minimize the plant's invasiveness in native habitats while providing nourishment at the table by incorporating it into regular mealtime.

How to Use This Book on Your Journey

This book covers wild edibles that I believe you will find delicious or useful. You will be guided through the seasons to learn what is edible when, what edible plant parts are best used in the kitchen, and how to harvest and prepare them. You'll also learn what plants to avoid completely.

In each entry, you will also learn about the plant's flavor and how to best prepare it, and why that flavor is helpful for optimal health. You'll gain a deeper understanding and appreciation for expanding the flavors currently at the dinner table with wild foods.

Watch for Cautions

While each plant showcased in this guide is relatively safe, any cautions or concerns will also be provided. Remember: you must be certain in your plant identification. And as with introducing any new food or herb into your diet, do so with care to eliminate any potential for adverse reactions.

What Regions Are Covered

I have chosen to feature plants that can be found across most the Midwest's ecologically diverse bioregions—from the prairie to the woodlands and the dunes habitats on the shores of the Great Lakes. While plant distributions don't keep to geopolitical boundaries on a map, this book includes plants from Illinois, Indiana, Iowa, Kansas, Michigan, Minnesota, Missouri, Nebraska, North Dakota, Ohio, South Dakota, and even the immediate region of Ontario.

This book will also help you to identify areas that are safe and suitable for foraging. You will learn to view foraging not only as a way to procure free food, but also as a sort of partnership with the land, keeping the sustainability of plant populations top of mind so the land can continue to nourish us for years to come.

A Focus on Sustainability

I have a strong affinity for wild, invasive, weedy plants and love to teach people how to rely on them for food. In addition to being pesky and abundant, these weeds have tremendous virtues, despite their condemnation. Wild and weedy plants are resilient, tolerating tough growing conditions. They are the wild varieties of plants that are commonplace in the grocery store and remain very true to their original genetics, never modified by a grower or in a lab. Invasive weeds make up most of my foraging, and I include many of my favorites here in this book.

Perhaps you'll be enticed to allow your own lawn and green spaces to re-wild themselves into edible, wild salad beds. To help encourage this, I have made a special mention if a plant is suited to an edible landscape or permaculture plan. Additionally, many edible plants that we include in landscape design are often overlooked as valuable potential harvests for the forager. Frequently fruit, flowers, leaves, and berries go unharvested in common areas and in parks. These are bounties just waiting to be noticed and enjoyed. I will show you where to find these, too.

Herbal Remedies and Safety

In this book, the plants I include and list as herbal remedies are ones I use personally with my own family and in my community herbalism practice. These plants are relatively safe and don't require significant caution or indications beyond what I've included in this book—unless it's specifically noted within the plant entry itself.

To that end, not all plants are suitable for use by all people in all situations as herbal medicine. It is your responsibility to learn more about the individual plants themselves and how they work with your needs, your body, and your current health status. For specific guidance, seek the support and consultation of a local herbalist in your area to determine herbal remedies that are best for you and your family's needs.

To Learn More

To hone your plant identification skills, seek out a multitude of resources. No field guide or resource is exhaustive, not even this one. Collect many plant guides. Libraries, nature centers, botanical gardens, and used bookstores are always good sources for botanical references, as is the internet. Visit the back of this book for more recommendations on other good sources of botanical and wild food resources.

Beginning Your Foraging Journey

As a forager and herbalist, I am often asked "What's outside now that I can forage or harvest?" or "How do I know what's edible?" or "Where do I start if I want to forage?" Here are some tips on getting started.

Get Outside

If you want to forage, you have to get outside. Being a forager and working with wild plants requires that you not only get to know the land and plants that live around you, but that you also must pay attention to the cycles of the year, the weather, and the bloom times of the wild plants.

The only way to do this is to be outside, year-round, paying attention with all five senses.

With this field experience (and as a life-long gardener), I am able to interpret the subtle changes in the weather and how that might affect a wild rose harvest or a gathering of delicate blackberries from the field before a rainstorm. This is a skill that you can and will develop as you spend more and more time outdoors observing and being in nature.

Wear gloves while gathering chestnuts—they are spiny!

You Are Here

Foraging, at its essence, is being able to rely on the wild plants that live around you. Frequently, new foragers will ask me for my foraging spots without ever having taken time to learn more about the plants in their immediate neighborhood. This always surprises me, because so many wild edible plants live right outside their own front doors. Pay attention to the plants that live around *you*. With a field guide, sketchbook, and perhaps a camera in hand, document the plants that you see.

Draw a map of your area by hand. Then check out your locale in Google Maps and take note of significant geological structures like lakes, streams, and forests, as well as manmade constructs in your community like highways and factories. This is where *you* live and where you will most likely do your day-to-day harvesting.

Use this map as a tool to track your progress and record your finds. Take it along on regular walks, and bring a friend, your kids, or a co-worker with you, too. Talk about what plants and seasonal changes you notice; ask a neighbor what he or she has seen as well. Take pictures to help you remember what you see; or better yet, have a set of colored pencils and paper in hand to sketch discoveries along your route. Photography and drawing will help you gain a more intimate knowledge of plants and help dedicate their botanical details to memory.

Intentionally take time to really notice all that is growing. Make note of the weather, the time of day, and season. Add the plants you notice to your map. Don't get caught up in learning their names at first. Just collect photos and drawings, and take plant clippings if you need to, and from there start your identification process.

And this is all before you gather—or certainly eat—any wild plants.

Keep Sustainability in Mind

As foragers, we are land stewards. Working with plants requires we understand not just their botany, but their abundance in our bioregions. It's important to know whether a plant is endangered or invasive (of course, the latter are better to harvest from a sustainability standpoint). It's also important to know how to carefully harvest a plant so it can continue to reproduce for future harvests and enjoyment. In each plant profile, I make note of how to safely harvest the plants so as to not impact the plant's population and to ensure future harvests.

Get to know the various habitats in your area, from hardwood deciduous forest to wetlands to urban lots. Over time, you will gain an intimate knowledge of their microclimates and what lives there, and you will come to understand what might be threatened or limited in amount.

Remember: foraging isn't about free forest food for the taking. It's about relationships with the plants around us. Do no harm, and leave the places from which we harvest in better shape than they were when we found them.

Get Permission

Unless you're in your own front yard, be sure you have legal permission to gather. Municipal, state, and federal parks all have various rules about foraging, hunting, and gathering. As these activities have become popular pastimes, it is best to start working with local-level park management staff as a land advocate on sustainable harvesting. Work together to cultivate ways to sustainably use more prolific and "noxious" weedy plants as food.

If you would like to search on private land, of course, you always must get permission. It's good karma to ask rather than trespass. Ask the owner to go along with you, and you might even make a new friend.

Something else to think about: in many cultures and native traditions that work with wild plants, there is reverence given when harvesting, and it is commonplace to ask the plant for its permission to harvest. This is done with a sense of respect and gratitude, and there is always an answer from the plants, if we foragers choose to ask and then listen to the answer.

"Rampant" Overharvesting: Don't Dig the Leeks

Ramps, the popular wild leek.

The wild leek, or ramps, has become a desirable foodie staple, popular on restaurant menus and in greenmarkets. But careless gathering now threatens the plant's future.

Recently, the wild leek (*Allium tricoccum*) has been the forager's darling, but this increase in popularity is putting pressure on the wild leek population along the East Coast and has the potential to do so in the Midwest. It takes about three years for a seed to develop into a mature leek ready for harvest—a long time!

I won't lie: I really love ramps. But unless we take some pressure off the plant population, we will ensure their demise.

This also brings up a larger issue of ethics when it comes to monetary gain from foraging. Chefs are paying foragers top dollar for the leeks—upward of $15 per pound in more affluent markets and restaurants. It is very tempting to take advantage of the market demand and look past the sustainable harvest of leeks. This isn't an issue exclusive to leeks: native plants like American ginseng and goldenseal are overharvested and traded on the black market for their medicinal values. So whether gathering wild plants for food or medicine, give the plant's distribution serious consideration before harvesting.

Safety Before All Else

Before you consider collecting your very first plant, you must be able to correctly identify the plant and understand any potentially hazardous growing conditions.

Know Thy Plants

It's wise, for many reasons, to positively identify plants before you do any tasting or harvesting. This is respectful of the

Basic Leaf Arrangements

If you are new to field botany, fear not! Trust that as you spend time observing plants, you will be able to more easily identify key botanical features—leaves, reproductive parts, flowers, and so on—and thus become more and more able to incorporate botanical language into your own plant vernacular. For starters, here are a few leaf arrangements that will be helpful in plant identification.

Alternate

Solomon's seal exhibits an alternate leaf pattern.

Compound

Elder has a compound leaf and umbel-shaped flowerhead.

Opposite

Motherwort is an example of a plant with opposite leaves and a square stem.

Circular Basal Rosette

Dandelion is a fine example of a circular basal rosette.

Lance-shaped, Toothed

Spearmint has a toothed, lance-shaped leaf.

Whorled

Cleavers' leaves grow in a circular whorled pattern up the stem.

This red clover is growing in an abandoned urban industrial lot in Detroit. Because of the likelihood of heavy metal contaminants (potentially lead), I would certainly avoid collecting plants like red clover that take up minerals and heavy metals from sites like this one.

plant and can prevent you from becoming seriously ill from harvesting the wrong plant or eating the wrong plant part. Safety first!

Don't try to cheat your way through plant identification. You might suspect you know a certain plant, and it's easy to skip over the details of an official description and make the plant fit your guess. But the skill of an adept forager is predicated on being positive about all details.

Watch for Soil Contamination

As a city-dwelling forager, I take the potential for soil contamination pretty seriously. It's easy to come across land, particularly in urban areas, that has excess lead or other pollutants that can be absorbed into plants. And soil contamination isn't just a concern for city folk. Rural and suburban soil contamination is also possible.

Knowing where to harvest and understanding which plants and plant parts may be more likely to contain contaminants such as heavy metals or environmental pollutants are the first steps to ensure safety. A gardener might have her soil tested before planting a garden bed, but it's likely that most foragers won't be soil testing in areas where they are collecting plants. If you are unfamiliar with the soil's history, it is usually best to find a different gathering location. Here are some other tips to gather plants safely in urban, suburban, and rural areas.

Know the History of the Land

First and foremost, know the history of the land on which you want to gather and what possible contaminants may be present. Ask the landowner and neighbors, and/or study public records.

Avoid harvesting along railroad tracks. These places are known to be high in arsenic, which can be absorbed into the plants.

Utility companies frequently use herbicides to keep easements free of trees and plants. Avoid these areas while foraging.

Other areas of land that you should consider carefully include:

Suburban zones Excess residual herbicide and pesticides may be present on lawns, golf courses, and corporate landscapes.

Urban zones Heavy metals like lead or other industrial pollutants may be present in areas that were once heavily industrialized; current brownfields (zones of heavily polluted areas as designated by the United States Environmental Protection Agency); old refuse and landfill sites, railroad tracks (arsenic); and old gas station sites. There is always room for concern over general pollution from particulates from brake dust and exhaust along heavily trafficked areas.

Agricultural zones Rural areas are as suspect for contaminants as urban areas. Factory farms can be sources of excess nitrates, fertilizers, and manure runoff. The presence of manure adds a possible source of watershed contamination like E. coli and salmonella. This is particularly important when you are considering plants that grow in wetlands or in a riverbed, downstream from a farm.

Corporate pollution Pharmaceutical companies, manufacturing, furniture industry, and paint companies are all potential environmental polluters, especially of heavy metals.

Municipal pollution Water treatment facilities can sometimes have raw sewage overloads, contributing to E. coli and salmonella loads in waterways. Power facilities can dump residual by-products (including graywater from the power-making process) into nearby waterways.

Public easements Herbicides are often used on easements to maintain clear access to power lines and other municipal services. Usually there is no public notice when the easements are treated; however, it's easy to spot herbicidal treatment as it produces a brown area that looks like it has been burned.

Roadways In winter, roadways are often treated with a salt or bromide solution,

Avoid harvesting in the immediate vicinity or downstream of an open water treatment plant like this one in South Dakota. The watershed and plants themselves can be easily contaminated with water-borne pathogens like *E. coli*.

and increasingly popular is the use of fracking solution to desalinate the roads. All these cause plant material to appear burned and dead during the growing season.

Irrigation on landscapes Graywater frequently used in irrigation has a potential for water-borne bacteria to exist, and simply washing plants in the kitchen cannot eliminate pathogens like *E. coli* and salmonella.

All Plants and Parts are Different

Not all plants and plant parts take up contamination in the same way so remember—any plant that we eat for its mineral content (dock, nettle, or lamb's quarters for example) can also take up and synthesize heavy metals like lead. And every plant and plant part behaves differently. For example, the flowers of elder gathered in a hedgerow of an urban park will most likely will have no significant concentration of heavy metals. A plant like curly or yellow dock, however, which is high in minerals like iron,

growing in an area where commercial manufacturing has taken place, very may well have significant trace amounts of lead or other heavy metal. To that end, I'd be hesitant about gathering a plant like dock at all—particularly the plant's roots—where heavy metals may exist. Ultimately, if you have suspicions or are uncertain in any way about a specific place, find another place to gather.

A Forager's Harvesting and Preservation Kit

As a forager, you need tools that allow you to comfortably and successfully gather wild foods and get them back to the kitchen for cleaning and preservation. Your toolkit will vary depending on the plants you want to harvest.

Gear for the Field

Each plant profile in this book notes any special tools you may need for the harvest, but in general your kit should contain:

Hand tools Digging forks, small hand

Having the right tools and equipment as part of your collection kit will make your foraging adventure easier and much more enjoyable. Shallow trays and baskets like these, for example, will help prevent berries from being crushed as they would in a deeper basket or bag.

trowels, loppers, hori-hori, kitchen shears, pruners, handsaw, leather gloves

Specialty tools Nut gatherers, nut-cracker, tweezers

Containers Berry baskets, shallow trays, buckets, burlap sacks, cotton market bags of various sizes, paper lunch sacks for smaller harvests

Botanical ID materials Plant identification books, camera, sketch pad, hand loupe, ruler, scissors, small plastic or paper bags for gathering samples of plants to identify at your desk

Dress for Success

My father would always say, "There is never the wrong weather, only the wrong clothing." In the Midwest, the weather switches on a dime, and as a forager's work is done mostly outside, be sure to dress for it. Not being prepared for the climate or weather changes can turn a foraging adventure into an uncomfortable or even unsafe walkabout. Here are some tips to remember (in no particular order):

→ Depending on the season, wearing the right layers will keep you happy and safe—cool, lightweight layers for summer, mid-weight layers for fall, and additional warmer layers for winter. And keep in mind, long pants can keep away scrapes, poison ivy, and insects (especially ticks).

→ Sensible footwear means something different to each person. Some like barefoot gear, others like a solid boot, and yet others prefer their tennis shoes or outdoor sandals. Whatever is comfortable to you is fine. But make it something other than flip-flops—poison ivy doesn't discriminate, and sunburned feet are a drag.

→ Pack hydration and a snack, or even a light picnic. There will be times where your planned one-hour walk turns into three. This isn't a problem if you've packed adequate water (especially in summer). And no one likes the classic "hangry" foraging partner who has low blood sugar and didn't pack a snack.

→ Consider traveling with a basic first aid kit, including bug spray (there are many natural blends you can make from wild catnip and yarrow). Chances are you won't need a full first aid kit for a neighborhood walk, but for day hikes, it's always nice to have something on hand for the bug bites, scrapes, and other basic mishaps.

→ Travel with common sense. Depending on the length of your adventure, ask yourself where you will be going. This will dictate what clothing and gear you need. If you are staying local, a GPS-enabled smartphone may be all you need. For day hikes in unfamiliar areas, be sure you have any needed trail or topography maps. Having a communication device is always smart, as is telling someone where you are going and when they can expect you home.

Back to the Kitchen

When you return home with your harvest in hand, you will want to have a well-stocked pantry to process your harvest. Being prepared will ensure that the results of your hard efforts in the field won't spoil on the counter waiting to be processed and preserved.

When you return to preserve the harvest, have the right pantry staples on hand so that your bounty can be kept at its freshest. Raw honey is a prime staple in my own pantry for helping preserve the wild harvests.

It's in every forager's interest to keep costs low in setting up (and replenishing) their food preservation kits. Procuring second-hand equipment like canners, funnels, ladles, measuring cups, and jars (new lids are required with each new batch of preserves) whenever possible is awesome. Resale shops, garage and estate sales, and even grandmas are great sources to help round out your preservation kit. A well-stocked preservation pantry should include:

→ Canning jars with new sealing lids
→ Funnels
→ Twine
→ Paper bags
→ Dehydrators
→ Screens for drying
→ Canners, pans, teakettle
→ Tongs, ladles, spoons
→ Vinegars
→ Olive oil
→ Raw honey
→ Sugar
→ Salts (rock salt, pickling salts, sea salts)
→ Liquors (mescal, tequila, vodka, grape liquors, mead, wine)
→ Homebrew supplies (carboys, yeasts, thermometers, buckets, siphons)

Savor Your Seasonal Harvest

Share your harvests with family and friends. Taste deeply the spicy garlic mustard pesto you've prepared, spreading it onto a crunchy yellow dock seed cracker topped with local goat cheese, while sipping a local Pinot Gris. Remember the weather when you harvested the foods— the sun, the wind, the smell of the soil.

This book contains many fun ways to use wild edibles. You will only be limited by your imagination, and perhaps, time. As a busy working mom, I know what it means to be overwhelmed with projects, especially when I try to make as many things as possible from scratch.

While you peruse this book and get ideas for your harvest year, don't get too overwhelmed or discouraged at the labor it entails to start to gather and cook wild foods into your regular meals, especially if you are new to foraged foods. Bit by bit, add the wild foods into your meals: top sandwiches with handfuls of wild greens, or make simple wild greens pestos for easy appetizers. Add in wild foods where you can and just have fun.

And with that—get outside!

Foraging the Finest of the Season: A Harvesting Guide

Just as a gardener knows the right time for planting and reaping a harvest, a forager must know the timing of wild plants just as intimately—knowing how they grow, when the plant is prime for harvest, and what weather is best for the harvesting.

Like a garden's growing season, wild plants also have a similar season. Wild greens are most tender in the early spring and then become tough and go to flower in hotter weather. The fruiting bushes, shrubs, and trees flower in spring and then yield succulent berries, most sweet under the hot summer sun. Bark from the trees is most easily gathered in the spring or fall, or from the fallen branches that rest on the forest floor after a wild summer storm.

What follows is a simple outline of the seasons and their plants that will help you learn the seasonal patterns of wild plants. It should help guide you on your walkabouts.

Take note that one plant's bloom time in one part of the Midwest can be very different from another elsewhere. Not only does the region of the Midwest cover a good deal of territory (the growing season of South Dakota is significantly shorter than that of southern Ohio, for instance), it is filled with microclimates with varying elevation, soil, and even weather (especially around the Great Lakes).

Early Spring

As the snow melts back from the fields and woodlands, the early greens of spring begin to poke through the ground. Many wild leafy greens are best gathered in the cooler weather of early spring before they grow larger and the increasing heat of the spring and summer changes their flavor. Edible tree leaves are also best harvested at this time as they are both tiny and tender.

Early spring greens are more tender—even with a hint of sweetness—and can be eaten fresh in salads. This is particularly true of bitter greens like garlic mustard, dock, dandelion, and chicory. As spring progresses into summer, greens grow larger and become significantly bitter, where they are best used as sautéed greens or cooked into frittatas. Use your senses to compare their flavors between the early and later months of the growing season and prepare them accordingly.

Fiddleheads unfurling in the early spring.

Early spring is also an excellent time to gather tree bark, twig tips, and small branches for making tea and herbal remedies, as the sap is still running through the tree, which makes the bark easier to process. Tubers, roots, rhizomes, and fiddleheads should also be gathered at this time, before the plants begin to move significant energy upward to grow stems, leaves, and flowers.

Where to Find Early Spring Plants

Full Sun: Open Fields, Disturbed Open Spaces, Edges of the Woods

amaranth leaves

asparagus shoots

basswood leaves

chickweed stems, leaves,
   flowers

chicory leaves, roots

dandelion leaves, flowers,
   roots

dock seeds, leaves, roots

Japanese knotweed shoots

juniper needles, berries

kudzu shoots, leaves, tubers

lamb's quarters leaves

mallow leaves, stems, root

ox-eye daisy leaves

peppermint leaves, stems

plantain leaves

raspberry leaves

redbud leaves, flowers

salsify leaves, shoots

wild lettuce leaves

Wetlands, Riverbeds, Lakeside

angelica root, leaves

cattail shoots, rhizome

nettle leaves

watercress leaves, stems

Woodlands and Partial Shade

aspen bark

beech leaves

black cherry bark, flowers

chaga fruiting body

cleavers leaves, stems,
   flowers

daylily tubers, shoots

field garlic bulb, stems,
   leaves

garlic mustard roots, leaves,
   flowers

greenbrier shoots, rhizomes

ostrich fern fiddleheads

Solomon's seal shoots, roots

spicebush twigs

spring beauty leaves, flowers

spruce needles, tips

sugar maple sap

trout lily leaves

white lettuce leaves

white pine needles, tips

wild ginger roots

wild leek leaves

wild onion bulb, leaves

wild sarsaparilla root

wintergreen leaves

wood sorrel leaves

yellow birch bark, sap

Mid- to Late Spring

In mid-spring, the temperature and soil begin to warm. The early spring plants send up flower stalks, and the summer perennials unfurl their first leaves. This is a perfect time to begin gathering tender leaves and flowers for teas, herbal remedies, and simple syrups.

Dandelions and redbud blossoms dot the landscape at the peak of springtime.

Where to Find Mid- to Late Spring Plants

Full Sun: Open Fields, Disturbed Open Spaces, Edges of the Woods

amaranth leaves

basswood flowers

blackberry leaves

burdock shoots

catnip leaves

chickweed stems, leaves, flowers

chicory root, leaves

dandelion leaves, flower, root

ground ivy leaves, flowers

juniper needles, berries

kudzu shoots, leaves, tubers

lamb's quarters leaves, stems

lemon balm leaves, stems, flowers

lilac flowers

mallow leaves, roots

milkweed shoots, buds

monarda leaves

motherwort leaves

mulberry fruit

ox-eye daisy flowers

pea shoots, flowers

pennycress leaves, seeds

peppermint leaves

pineapple weed leaves, flower head

plantain leaves

poke shoots

prickly pear pads

salsify leaves, root, stems, flowers

tulip poplar flowers, twigs

violet leaves, flower

wild carrot leaves

wild grape leaves

wild strawberry fruit

wormwood leaves

yarrow leaves

Wetlands, Riverbeds, Lakeside

angelica root, leaves

cattail rhizome, shoots, stalk

cow parsnip leaves

horsetail stems

nettle leaves

spearmint leaves

Woodlands and Partial Shade

black locust flowers

chaga fruiting body

cleavers leaves

jewelweed leaves, stems

spicebush twigs, leaves

white lettuce leaves

wild ginger roots

wild onion bulb, leaves, flowers

wintergreen leaves, berries

wood sorrel leaves

Summer

Summer is a magical time in the woods and fields in the Midwest. The smells of sweet clover fill the air, crickets chirp, and in the evening, lightning bugs fill the sky. Foraging harvests are bountiful, especially with all of the fruits and berries. The wild greens are more bitter this time of year, but will return again in abundance in the fall.

Goldenrod is abundant in the sunny, open fields of summertime.

Where to Find Summer Plants

Full Sun: Open Fields, Disturbed Open Spaces, Edges of the Woods

amaranth leaves

blackberry leaves, fruit, root

blueberry fruit

catnip leaves, flower

chicory leaves, flowers, roots

currant fruit

dock leaves, seeds

goldenrod flowers, leaves

hibiscus flowers

honeysuckle flowers

huckleberry fruit

hyssop flowers, leaves

kudzu shoots, leaves, tubers

lamb's quarters leaves

milkweed flowers, pods

monarda flowers, leaves

ox-eye daisy flowers

pea shoots, pods

pennycress leaves, seeds

pineapple weed flowers,
    stems

purslane leaves, stems,
    flowers

raspberry leaves, fruit, root

redbud pods

red clover leaves, flowers

rose flowers

sassafras leaves

serviceberry berries

spotted bee balm flowers,
    leaves

sweet clover leaves, flowers

white clover leaves, flowers

wild carrot flowers, roots,
    seeds

wormwood leaves

yarrow leaves, flowers

Wetlands, Riverbeds, Lakeside

angelica flowers, seeds,
    leaves, root

cattail pollen, stalks

cow parsnip leaves, stems

elder flowers, berries

Woodlands and Partial Shade

black cherry fruit

black walnut green hulls

blueberry fruit

chaga fruiting body

daylily tubers, shoots, flowers

groundnut tubers

huckleberry fruit

jewelweed leaves, stems,
    flowers

thimbleberry fruit

wintergreen leaves,
    berries

wood sorrel leaves

Fall

Fall is a very special harvest season for the forager. Tender greens like dock, nettle, and dandelion are again tender and more sweet with the reappearance of the cooler weather. Fruits like apples, pears, and cranberries can be gathered in abundance and processed into chutneys, jams, and sauces. Some foods, like rose hips and wild grapes, are better to gather after the first frost, as falling temperatures increase the sugars and sweeten the fruit.

A harvest of wild apples and pears, a quintessential fall foraging find on trails and in old orchards.

Nuts fall everywhere: acorns, chestnuts, hazelnuts, and beechnuts can be collected by the sackful. Roots, tubers, and rhizomes can also be dug and preserved as pickles, and the last of the summer's herbs and flowers can be collected before the frosts and snow arrive.

Where to Find Fall Plants

Full Sun: Open Fields, Disturbed Open Spaces, Edges of the Woods

American persimmon fruit
apple fruit
autumn olive fruit
blackberry fruit
burdock roots
chickweed leaves, stems
chicory roots
crabapple fruit
dandelion roots
dock leaves, root
ginkgo leaves, nuts
goldenrod flowers

groundcherry fruit
hawthorn fruit
juniper needles, berries
kousa dogwood fruit
kudzu tubers
lemon balm leaves
mallow leaves, root
monarda leaves
peppermint leaves
pineapple weed leaves,
    flowers
plantain leaves

prickly pear fruit
rose hips
salsify leaves, roots
sumac berries
sunchoke tubers
violet leaves, flowers
wild carrot root, seeds
wild grape fruit
wild peach fruit
wild pear fruit
wild plum fruit

Wetlands, Riverbeds, Lakeside

angelica root
cranberry fruit

horsetail stems
nettle leaves

spearmint leaves
wild rice rice

Woodlands and Partial Shade

aspen bark
beech nuts
black walnut nuts
chaga fruiting body
chestnut nuts
field garlic bulb, leaves
greenbrier rhizomes

groundnut tubers
hazelnut nuts
hickory nuts
oak acorns
pawpaw fruit
Solomon's seal roots
spicebush berries, twigs,
    leaves

wild sarsaparilla root
wintergreen leaves
wood sorrel leaves
yellow birch bark, leaves

Winter

In the Midwest, most of us are used to many feet of snow blanketing the ground in winter and don't normally think of it as a foraging season. But microclimates and ebbs and flows in winter weather

Maple sap begins to run in the depths of winter while the rest of the earth is still quiet and blanketed with snow.

allow for certain plants to be easily accessed and gathered even during this season. Before the ground thoroughly freezes, roots can still be gathered. Before the wet, damp rains turn to snow, aromatic stalks of summer's flowers can still be accessed for plant medicines and teas (use your sense of smell and taste to decide how potent the aromatics still are).

Winter is also a useful time to practice plant identification. Take particular notice of tree bark, the stalks of last season's plants, and dried berries on bushes and vines—these are all clues that can assist you in better learning and identifying plants for next season's foraging adventures.

Where to Find Winter Plants

Full Sun: Open Fields, Disturbed Open Spaces, Edges of the Woods

monarda leaves	rose hips

Woodlands and Partial Shade

chaga fruiting body	sugar maple sap	wintergreen leaves
field garlic leaves	white pine needles	yellow birch sap

Wild Edible Plants
of the Midwest

The Midwest has a variety of ecosystems from which a forager can gather a bountiful harvest. Here, an old farmstead is slowly reclaimed by the wild bushes and trees in the hedgerows, offering wild fruits, berries, and wild plants for the forager's enjoyment.

amaranth

Amaranthus species

EDIBLE leaves, seeds

Amaranth is a versatile, weedy plant that is easy to locate and identify. It tastes like mild spinach, and its leaves can be cooked in a variety of delicious ways that will provide plant proteins, carbohydrates, vitamins, and minerals such as calcium, iron, and potassium.

How to Identify

In the Midwest, several species of *Amaranthus* can be found in areas of disturbed soil that have plenty of moisture and sunlight, in empty lots, fields, farmland, and drainage areas or river floodplains. Tall and weedy, amaranth grows 6 to 8 feet tall, depending on growing conditions and soil.

The leaves are a dull army green, about 2 to 5 inches long, and have an oval or lanceolate shape. Soft and tender when young, the leaves and stems are tough and dry to

Amaranth greens are delicious when the leaves are still small and tender; but because they are not excessively bitter, they can also be enjoyed cooked in summer when the leaves mature.

the touch later in the season. The flower cluster, which has both male and female flowers, can be up to 12 inches long. In fall, the cluster can bow under the weight of the seeds.

Where and When to Gather

Amaranth is an annual plant. Harvest tender greens in early to mid-spring. By mid- to late summer, the plant will have grown tall and tough and have already gone to seed. It's common for amaranth to thrive in disturbed areas, particularly in the city, around developments, and in farmland areas. As amaranth is mineral-dense, it can also take up lead and nitrates that may be present in the soil into its stem and leaves. Harvest in an area where you are familiar with soil quality.

How to Gather

Choose small, tender leaves and stems that look vibrant and are not affected by bug damage or blight. Larger leaves of the plant are still edible, however, but will be noticeably dry and tough.

Seeds ripen and dry in late summer into early fall and can be collected by hand. Gather these before fall rains arrive to ensure a dry, clean seed free of mildew and mold, and winnow the seeds from their bracts carefully, as some species can be spiny and catch on the mouth and throat if not removed.

How to Eat

Amaranth is not bitter like the leaves of the chicories or dandelion. Its leaves and tender stems are best prepared as cooked greens. They cook down quite a lot, so gather a few fresh handfuls per serving. As the plant has a slightly rough texture on the tongue, it isn't ideal eaten raw. Also, cooking the greens helps make the minerals more bioavailable. Soups, sautés, quiches, baked vegetable dishes—all are suitable for amaranth greens. The greens can be cooked as a replacement for chard or spinach, or can be blanched and frozen for later use.

The seeds have a nutty flavor similar to the cultivated amaranth found on the grocery store shelf and are as nutrient dense, but must be cooked (or soaked) in order for you to benefit from the minerals, vitamins, and plant proteins. The seeds can be roasted or toasted, and they serve as a nice addition to salads, homemade multi-grain crackers, and granola.

Toasted or cooked amaranth seeds can be processed into flour and added to a flour mix. However, its flour does not contain gluten and will not result in a light, fluffy loaf of bread. The seeds can also add amazing plant protein to any homemade energy bar or granola mix, good for the athlete or active person who wants a locally grown, nutrient-dense wild food addition to his or her training regime. Amaranth seeds make a delicious morning porridge topped with maple syrup.

Future Harvests

The heavy seed heads of the amaranth disperse seed across open fields and disturbed areas of land. It is prolific and regenerates easily. Overharvesting does not seem to be a significant problem with amaranth.

American beech

Fagus grandifolia

EDIBLE leaves, nuts

American beech is a grand tree and hardwood source, but you can also enjoy its early leaves and nutrition-packed nuts for baking and in foraged chai teas with other gathered herbs.

How to Identify

Where once the American beech was abundant across the eastern seaboard and Midwest, this grand tree is now most common in mixed hardwood forests, often found with maple and oak trees in rich, well-drained soil. The American beech can reach heights upward of 120 feet with diameters of 4 to 5 feet across.

The bark is a steely smooth blue-gray, and the vibrant green and shiny leaves grow to be 2 to 5 inches long and are ovate,

Beech leaves in early spring.

Beechnut harvest.

serrated, and slightly toothed. They change to an opaque cream color in winter—some call them ghost leaves—and stay on the branches long into the cold season, which makes the tree easy to identify then.

Beech flowers in late spring. Its tannic nut is borne in a prickly husk, which ripens and falls from the tree from September to November. The nutmeat is found within the distinctively pyramidal shell.

Where and When to Gather

In early spring, gather the leaves for spring greens. When the American beech matures at about 40 years old, it begins to produce nut crops every three to five years. The nut develops in a prickly husk and falls from the tree in mid- to late fall. Your competition will be local wildlife, which particularly enjoy this nut. So when the nuts start to fall, gather fast.

How to Gather

The tender leaves of the beech can be gathered right after they begin to leaf out in early spring. Gather the ripened nut from the tree or from windfall on the ground, taking care to choose nuts that are plump and free of mold or insect damage. Crack the pyramidal shell and extract the nutmeat for cooking.

Beech tree in winter with "ghost" leaves—a chief identifier of the tree in winter, along with its smooth and gray bark.

How to Eat

Use the early, young, and tender leaves of the American beech in a wild greens salad along with other early spring foraged greens, including the young leaves of the American basswood, dandelion, violets, and garlic mustard. The nuts are a versatile winter food staple that can offer minerals such as potassium, vitamin B9 (folate), and omega 3 and omega 6 fatty acids.

Unlike the acorn, soaking and leaching the beechnut nutmeat in water isn't absolutely necessary before working with it in the kitchen. However, soaking the nut before roasting and grinding will aid in its digestibility. Roasting the nutmeat in an iron skillet will offer the nut a full-toasted flavor and is recommended, particularly if the nut will be used in a beverage.

Crush and boil the nuts to make a mineral-rich, nutty drink, and consider blending the beechnut beverage into a local nut chai or hot cocoa with hickory nuts. The soaked and roasted nut can also be ground and used in conjunction with other nuts like hickory and acorn to make a nut flour for baking.

Future Harvests

The mature American beech offers its nuts only every three to five years, so mature stands of beech are needed for a consistent source of nuts. Tree plantings and preserving mixed hardwood habitats are important to the future of the American beech.

American persimmon

Diospyros virginiana
winter plum
`EDIBLE` fruit

Foragers who enjoy the Asian persimmon will be delighted to know that the American persimmon can be found throughout the lower Midwest and that it can be enjoyed in the same delicious ways.

How to Identify

American persimmon is a common hardwood tree found across the lower Midwest and Southeast of the U.S. It's often used as an ornamental in formal gardens as it is shade- and drought-tolerant. The tree is also found in the wild on the edges of mixed hardwood forests or in the partial shade of thickets and along hedgerows. Its leaves are oblong, about 3 to 4 inches long, with smooth edges. The bark is gray, deeply furrowed, and plated.

Where and When to Gather

An unripe persimmon is undesirable: it's extremely astringent, and its tannins will make your mouth pucker and dry out. Ripe persimmons have a wrinkled skin that is soft to the touch; the flesh will be equally soft with a deeper yellow-orange color. Persimmons are ready in mid- to late fall.

How to Gather

Persimmons that fall easily to the ground or have fallen already are ready for eating. Those that are tightly attached to the twigs are still unripe. Avoid fruit with insect damage or broken skin.

American persimmon tree heavy with fruit.

Ripe persimmons ready for eating.

How to Eat

Wild-harvested American persimmon can be prepared similarly to a cultivated Asian persimmon. Persimmon puree can be turned into a fun fruit leather snack for kids (try using maple syrup as the sweetener), used as a topping for a brie cheese plate appetizer, or added to citrus-based smoothies. Persimmon puree can also be used in fruit breads, teacakes, and baked goods like scones or fruit bars. It can also be enjoyed atop yogurt or homemade ice cream.

Dried in a dehydrator and sliced, the persimmon can be integrated into granola or baked goods, or enjoyed simply as a snack. Fresh, roughly chopped persimmon can be cooked down on the stovetop with sugar, vinegar, and chili spices to make a warming Indian chutney. Change the flavors a bit, and then the cooked chutney base can be blended with other fruits to make a fruit salsa.

Future Harvests

A fruiting tree can produce several hundred fruit. Competition for the windfall will include local wildlife, a consideration when foraging for the fruits, but otherwise gathering the fruit will do little to impact future harvests.

angelica

Angelica atropurpurea

EDIBLE roots, leaves, stems, seeds

Angelica is a common herb with a long history of use and lore stretching back through the Middle Ages. Aromatic, spicy, and warming, angelica has an anise-like flavor. The entire plant can be prepared in a variety of ways for cooking, cocktail, and herbal remedy use.

How to Identify

Angelica is a member of the family Apiaceae, so it is important to distinguish it from the poisonous members of the group (particularly poison hemlock, *Conium maculatum*). The stalk of angelica is hollow, smooth, and purple. Leaves are ovate, with three leaflets that divide further into three to five segments on each leaflet. The blossoms of angelica are white-green and are arranged in globe-shaped, terminal assemblages that can range from 2 to 6 inches. They produce creamy white and beige broad, oval seeds. Its root is white

Angelica in the spring.

Angelica's ovate leaflets, purple stems, and globe-shaped flower arrangement are notably different from the leaves of wild carrot, cow parsnip, and poison hemlock. The entire plant should also smell aromatic like celery when crushed.

Angelica seeds are a delicious culinary spice. Grind dry angelica seeds and add to chai for a spicy, aromatic licorice and ginger-like flavor.

and gnarled, and smells strongly of celery. The spicy and acrid aroma and flavor is a chief defining identifier of angelica.

Where and When to Gather

Angelica grows in hedgerows and along the edges of the woods, usually in damp soil. It is frequently found in ravines, floodplains, ditches, and gullies. It can self-sow to create large stands and tolerates shade well. The plant shows its first leaves in the early spring, flowers in midsummer, and goes to seed and dies back toward late summer and early fall.

How to Gather

The entire plant of angelica can be used—from root to seed. It is easiest to harvest the plant when it matures in late summer or early fall, when the seeds are dry and ready for gathering. The roots can be dug, washed, and dried for later use. The leaves can be stripped from the stem and dried for tea. The seeds should be gathered in dry weather when fully ripe. At home, take additional time to ensure the seeds are dried before storage.

How to Eat

A warming, aromatic tea can be made from fresh or dry roots and leaves; flavor the tea with herbs like hyssop and sweeten it with honey. The tea can be savored to relieve a chill from cold, damp weather, and it can also soothe a stomachache or damp cough.

The fresh stalks can be chopped and candied in cane sugar for use in confections or eaten alone as a candy treat, similar to candied ginger. The root can also be candied like this, as well as extracted (see sidebar) or prepared as a simple syrup to flavor sodas or cocktails.

The seeds can be nibbled after a meal as a digestive aid to settle an upset stomach. They are spicy and aromatic, and can also be ground into a spice to add to a warming chai.

Making and Using a Culinary Plant Extract

Plant extracts (also called tinctures in herbal medicine) are liquid preparations of plants that are made to extract flavors, resins, aromatics, and other medicinal constituents. Examples of common and commercially available plant extracts in culinary use are vanilla or almond extract. In this book, I offer many suggestions for making plant extracts for cocktail bitters and as culinary flavoring agents.

To make a plant extract, either fresh or dry plant material can be used along with a liquid solvent (also called menstruum in herbal medicine), usually a vodka or grape brandy, but a high-proof grain alcohol, mead, wine, or vinegar can also be used, depending on the desired final product. Glycerin is another possibility, in some cases, as a substitute for alcohol, but the texture and sweetness will affect the final product. In selecting your menstruum, remember that high-proof alcohol will best extract resins, and vinegars will best extract minerals from plants. But in most cases, using an affordable (that is, cheap) 40 percent alcohol vodka is perfectly acceptable in making common culinary extracts.

Making a plant extract for culinary use is simple. First, break down the plant material you are wishing to tincture—for example, chop roots, cut up leafy plants, grind aromatic seeds, and crush berries—and then pack the material into a canning jar to 50 percent of its volume if the plant is fresh, or 25 percent of volume if dry. Then, completely submerge the plant materials and top off the jar with your chosen solvent and make sure there is no air in the jar. Cover, shake, and store for at least a few weeks to allow full extraction of the plant's constituents. The finished extract should be strained and then bottled for use. Alcohol plant extracts can have a shelf life of three to five or more years if stored in a cool, dark place.

CAUTION These are the leaves of the poison hemlock, *Conium maculatum*. Notice how the leaf pattern is different from that of angelica, and poison hemlock will lack the spicy and aromatic smell of angelica. Do not touch the plant if you are unsure, as its neurotoxins can be carried into the body by way of the skin.

Future Harvests

While angelica can self-sow and take over in the right conditions, be sure to consider the impact on the size of angelica plantings if you are harvesting the plant for its roots. If you are harvesting a large quantity and are concerned about the population in the area, angelica can be propagated by transplants made with cuttings.

Caution

While angelica and poison hemlock (*Conium maculatum*) both can have purple coloring along their stalks, the entire plant of angelica is most certainly strongly aromatic of celery. If there is any doubt, however, do not crush the plant with your fingers (prior to smelling it) without wearing gloves, as the toxins in poison hemlock can be absorbed through the skin. Certainly do not taste it if you are unsure of the plant's identity.

apple

Malus species

fruit

Upon biting into a once-domesticated, now-wild apple, you will taste a broad range of flavors: sweet, tannic, astringent, cooling, and delicious—dynamic tastes, all too frequently missing from the few bland varieties featured in the supermarket.

How to Identify

Wild apple trees are found across the Midwest in fields and hedgerows. It is a small, fruiting tree, with brown, scaly bark and dense branches. Its leaves are ovate with serrated margins and a light-colored underside. The flowers of the apple tree are arranged in corymbs, each having five petals that range in color from pinkish white to white, with multiple stamens.

Where and When to Gather

Wild apple trees are very common on public land and hiking trails, particularly if the land was once an orchard or farmstead, a common occurrence in the fruit belt

Wild apples found off the beaten path, the fruit ripe for the picking and eating.

Wild apples are often found in old orchards or along trail routes in the fall.

area of the Midwest. Apple trees are also common as ornamentals, though are not extremely popular because many suburbanites and municipalities view the excess fruit as bothersome.

Being attuned to the apple's harvest time will help you select a well-ripened apple that has a nice aroma for eating, baking, and cider-making. The growing season will have an impact on the juice content in the flesh and its sugars, and other pest and blight considerations that often affect rose family plants also come into play.

The apple's fragrant blossoms attract many honeybees during mid- to late spring flowering. Fruits become ripe in mid- to late fall. As an apple ripens, its aromatics become more pronounced. The skins of the apple contain aromatic oils, acids, tannins (bitter and astringent substances), yeasts, and pigments high in antioxidants. An unripe apple's skin will be noticeably tannic. Allowing the apple to ripen closer to frost and gathering fallen fruit will ensure the most ripened sugars and aromatics.

How to Gather

Apples that detach easily from the tree and freshly fallen apples are most ripe. Choose apples that are free of insect damage as the fruit is frequently subject to resident caterpillars.

Gift from an Early Forager

Johnny Appleseed is the stuff of American folklore. John Chapman, Johnny's birth name, left his family's apple seedling nursery in Pennsylvania to move west. He took few possessions into the wilderness, just apple seeds and some traveling basics. Johnny Appleseed lived off the land and in return, made sure to plant small orchards wherever he landed in the clearing of woodland fields, allowing them minimal cultivation.

In the spirit of protecting the wilderness and of being a steward of natural resources, Johnny continued planting orchards in wild places until his death in 1845. Folklore has it that if you come upon a wild apple orchard in the wilderness, it can be traced back to the hands that planted these seeds in the early 19th century.

How to Eat

The simplest way to enjoy a wild apple is right off the tree, as a snack on your fall foraging explorations. Wild apple recipes are endless: from pies and jams to butters, sauces, and chutneys, the wild apple serves to delight in all of these ways. The pectin content in wild apples is much higher than in domesticated apples, so you can save cores and skins to make your own pectin concentrate from scratch.

If you are a cider enthusiast, wild apples yield a cider that is fresh, crisp, and dry. The wild apple's high tannin levels can make cider flavor profiles and aromatics in the final batch hard to predict. If your cider happens to go off, it can easily be finished off to make a fine homemade raw apple cider vinegar, which has many culinary and medicinal uses.

Future Harvests

Where once there were over 140,000 varieties of wild apples, now only a handful are available on the commercial market, and this has led to an American palate that now appreciates only a few of the apple's complexities of taste. It is of little concern if we overharvest their fallen fruits, though wildlife appreciates the windfalls, too.

asparagus
Asparagus officinalis

`EDIBLE` shoots

A favorite springtime vegetable, asparagus can be found in the wild as well as at the farmers market from early to late spring. Sautéed, steamed, roasted, pickled, or julienned fresh, foraged asparagus is as delicious as its cultivated counterpart.

How to Identify

It's easiest to begin seeking out wild asparagus in September and October, when it forms golden yellow bushes, thick with wispy, threadlike foliage. The woody stalks of the late-season asparagus will hold up through the winter and help mark the spot where you will find tender new shoots of asparagus in the early spring (usually late March in most Midwest locales, once snow thaw begins). The small shoots look similar to grocery store asparagus—dark green tips and stalks that grow and become woody and tall, with tiny, green flowers on branchlets that cluster in the axils of the leaves on the main stalk. The small, hard

Tender, young asparagus shoots are a delicious sign of early spring.

The feathery, bushy, and tall fronds of the wild asparagus help to easily identify the plant.

Asparagus fronds turn golden in the fall, making it easy to spot and map their location so you can return for the spring shoots.

red berries on the mature female plants are not edible.

Where and When to Gather

Perennial asparagus sends up shoots in early spring in sandy, well-drained soil, most often in abandoned fields and along sunny trails, ditches, and hedgerows. Look for new shoots at the base of last season's straw-colored, fallen bushes. They may be hard to spot under winter's leaf litter, but with a good eye out for the old fronds, you will be able to spot them.

How to Gather

Clip off the shoots with garden pruners or a sharp harvest knife, taking care to wash any sandy soil off the stalk before eating.

How to Eat

Wild asparagus can be prepared similarly to the cultivated variety found in the market. Choose tender shoots or peel the larger stalks. Take care to wash any sandy loam out of the tips. Then steam, sauté, or broil the stalks, or simply julienne and eat them raw in salads. Asparagus pickles nicely: an excellent springtime cocktail pickle could include the wild asparagus and the bulb of the wild leek. It's a perfect addition to a martini or bloody Mary.

Future Harvests

Wild asparagus is a perennial plant. The shoots are connected to the rootstock through a central crown, so it is important to trim—not pull—the tender springtime shoots from the plant so the rootstock remains intact and can produce shoots the following year.

aspen

Populus tremuloides
quaking aspen
`EDIBLE` bark

Aspen bark, combined with other herb flavors, has a complex dark aromatic flavor that lends itself well to a cocktail bitters, baking extract, and aromatic tea.

How to Identify

Aspen grows in large stands, interconnected to other trees via an underground root system, similar to that of a mushroom network. Stands of aspen can be located along stream banks and meadows, and are common at higher elevations. The bark of the aspen is notably green-gray, with triangular, heart-shaped, and smooth leaves that are known to "quake" or wave in the breeze because of their flat stems.

Where and When to Gather

Gather the tree bark of the aspen from newly fallen branches after a windstorm.

The bark of the aspen makes a delicious, aromatic cocktail bitters.

How to Gather

Aspen bark can be sustainably harvested by collecting twigs and tips from young saplings. Use your sense of smell and taste by chewing on a twig to discern its aromatics before gathering with kitchen shears or pruners.

Also, if you need a large quantity of inner bark, usually there are enough fresh wind-fallen branches after a spring storm within a stand of aspens to make harvesting the bark of a sapling or live tree unnecessary. Process the twigs and branches or inner bark into a plant extract (see angelica) or dry on a screen and store in a container when completely dry for later use.

How to Eat

Aspen bark can be made into a delicious cocktail bitter that works well with darker, spicy rums, and it even can be used to

Selecting and Processing Tree Bark

Using tree bark is a common practice among foragers and herbalists. In this book, I talk about gathering aspen, cherry, and yellow birch barks for culinary flavoring agents, but I also gather barks from willow, oak, cramp bark, witch hazel, and slippery elm, among others, for my herbal practice.

Gathering and stripping bark is fairly straightforward. Remember first that bark is easiest to gather from the tree in the early spring, when sap flows through the tree and makes the outer and inner bark peel from the inner cambium layer more easily.

If you are gathering small batches of bark for home use, there really is no reason to select a live tree. Seek out freshly cut trees or freshly fallen branches after a spring storm. Tree pruning is common in early spring: contact a local trimming service and tell them what specific tree you are looking for.

The tree grows with a protective outer bark and an inner bark; for most medicinal preparations, you'll want to gather the inner bark. Do this by cutting and scraping the outer bark vertically from the cambium center into strips and then scraping out the inner bark (methods will vary from tree to tree). Once removed, the inner bark can be used fresh or dried for later use. Store completely dry in a container.

I would also suggest a simpler process for making culinary extracts or teas of aromatic barks. In early spring, I frequently clip the new, young twigs and branch tips off live yellow birch, cherry, or aspen trees to make aromatic plant extracts or teas. I taste and chew the tips to get a sense of flavor. If the tips are aromatic, the twigs and tips can then be processed into a plant extract or dried and stored for later use.

Aspens grow in a connected stand, making them easy to identify from a distance. Their triangular, heart-shaped, and smooth leaves appear to wave to you from a distance because of their square stems, revealing their silvery gray underside.

flavor a gin cocktail. The aromatic alcohol extract of the aspen bark can be used in place of almond extract, lending a nice wild aromatic note to your baking projects.

The tea made from aspen bark is aromatic with a back note of almond. It blends well with sarsaparilla, spicebush, wild ginger, and sassafras leaf for an aromatic foraged chai tea. This warming, spicy tea can soothe a chill or ease indigestion caused by overindulgence, or can simply be enjoyed on a cold, fall day.

Future Harvests

Stands of aspen are quite prolific, but be mindful when bark harvesting: never remove the bark from the tree all the way around. Employ good technique (see page 54) and when possible, use fresh, fallen branches rather than stripping bark from a live tree.

autumn olive

Elaeagnus umbellata

EDIBLE berries

On a warm fall day, it is a true delight to stumble upon a bush of autumn olive berries (or more correctly, drupes) while hiking. The small and plentiful red berries are a perfect trail snack—tart and juicy enough to make your mouth pucker a bit and quench a parched throat, and balanced enough with a berry sweetness.

How to Identify

Once planted as a drought-tolerant ornamental, autumn olive is now widespread across the Midwest. Deemed by many preservationists as invasive to native ecosystems, this dense, deciduous, sprawling shrub is found in open spaces, along trails, and in disturbed areas. The autumn olive shrub thrives in full and part sun, attaining a height of up to 15 feet.

Its bark is gray and scaly, and the leaves are a dull dark green. The leaf growth is

Autumn olive berries are abundant in late summer and early fall in open fields and along trails. This delicious edible is deemed by many naturalists as an invasive species. Enjoy its delicious berries to your heart's delight.

Autumn olive in flower in spring.

alternate; leaves are oval and about 3 to 5 inches long with a smooth edge and silvery underside. The autumn olive blooms in late spring, with abundant fragrant yellow flowers that grow in clusters. The fruit of the autumn olive is small, about the size of a pea. It remains green, then ripens into a bright silvery red berry.

Where and When to Gather

The autumn olive fruits in late summer and early fall. The harvest can continue for several weeks until mid-November depending on the growing season. Gather fruits from shrubs in areas that have not been treated with an herbicide meant to eradicate the plant.

How to Gather

The silvery red berries that have swollen until they are almost spherical will be the sweetest; unripe green berries will be too tart, tannic, and astringent. A taste test will help you select the right bush to pick. If there is an unpleasant, astringent aftertaste, choose another bush from which to gather the fruit. The berries are small, but the shrubs offer an abundance on its branches. It shouldn't take too long to fill a bucket.

How to Eat

The autumn olive is a very versatile berry to work with in the kitchen. With its combination of sweet and tart, it shines in jam and fruit leather. But first, run the fruit through a food mill to remove the seeds.

Autumn olive is an invasive plant that often incites aggressive plant management by parks staff and gardeners.

The berries can also be frozen whole for winter kitchen projects. Don't overlook the autumn olive as a wonderful fresh fruit for the table: use the fruit to top salads, morning porridges, or even as a small side plate accompanying a variety of local cheeses in the place of domestic table grapes.

Future Harvests

Frequently, nature centers and local land conservancy organizations will clear stands of autumn olive bushes in the spring and fall as part of their habitat preservation programs. Aid their efforts: lend a hand clearing, and if it's fall, gather fruit at the same time.

basswood

Tilia species

linden

EDIBLE flowers, bracts, leaves, seeds

In early summer, basswood blossoms fill the air with a scent so sweet and strong that it is reminiscent of jasmine. Basswood's blossoms are a delicious offering. They can be used a fragrant, sweet syrup for sodas and cocktails or to make a soothing tea to calm upset nerves.

How to Identify

Basswood is well distributed across North America and can be found in all temperate climates across the Midwest. The tree grows wild in mixed hardwood forests, particularly in river floodplains in rich, well-drained soil. It is also common as an ornamental tree, planted in neighborhoods and urban areas by city planners.

The bark is dark gray and rough. It grows in long, flat-topped ridges that look like they have been smoothed with sandpaper.

Basswood flowers smell sweet like honeysuckle or jasmine, and make an amazing tea and aromatic simple syrup to flavor sodas and cocktails.

Basswood is a common tree planting in parks and cities. Here, the littleleaf linden offers shade to the business district in downtown Grand Rapids, Michigan. Note the spade-like shape of the upper branches and leaves, making the tree easy to identify in large plantings and stands, or even standing alone in a wooded area.

Basswood species can grow to heights reaching more than 80 feet. Its leaves are heart-shaped, toothed, and slightly hairy on both sides. The flowers are white with five petals that bloom in clusters below 2- to 3-inch-long strap-shaped bracts.

Where and When to Gather

Basswood starts to leaf out in early to mid-spring, and the leaves are edible as early season salad greens while still small and tender. Larger leaves are rough and unpleasant to eat. The tree blooms in early summer for about 10 days. Its blossoms fill the air with a sweet and rich scent reminiscent of jasmine. Use your nose at this time of year to seek out these fragrant blossoms; they make a fine tea and cocktail syrup. The fruits of basswood offer tiny, nut-like seeds in the fall. These are edible but are difficult to gather, crack open, and extract.

How to Gather

The honeybees will tell you when the blossoms are ripe for gathering: they fill the tree to gather the pollen and nectar. Take care as you will be sharing space with these busy herbalists as you gather the flowers.

The flowers and bracts can both be harvested by simply trimming the entire bract and cluster from the branch. They will be sticky (and so will your hands), so gather your harvest into a lint-free bag or basket.

How to Eat

For an early season salad green, the tender leaves of basswood are delicious while still small. The tea made with fresh and dry flowers and bracts is deliciously sweet and fragrant, with a mild honey-like taste and an aromatic note of jasmine. The tea is mild and is wonderful for soothing nerves.

The fresh flowers and bracts can also be made into a simple syrup with that similar honey-jasmine aromatic that serves as a delicious base for homemade sodas, to sweeten lemonade, or as a good cocktail ingredient. The syrup also freezes well for winter use.

Future Harvests

Basswood is a common native tree and landscape planting across the Midwest. Gathering flowers in a quantity suitable for household use and consumption would not disturb the balance of the distribution of this plant.

blackberry

Rubus species

EDIBLE berries, leaves, roots

The dark, jammy fruit of the blackberry is a forager's favorite midsummer find along a sunny trail. The plant offers an abundance of food: its leaves and roots can be used for tea, and the berry makes delicious eating.

How to Identify

Common in sandy, well-drained soils, blackberry is usually found as a large stand of plants in the sun on the edges of the wood. A bramble of a plant reaching heights to 5 feet, the blackberry is covered in thorns; its divided leaf clusters hold three to five serrated and ovate leaflets which have a prickly midrib. The blackberry blooms in late spring with white, five-petaled flowers that bear seedy, slightly hairy fruit that ripens into dark purple berries in late summer.

Blackberry fruit ripe in the summer sun.

Where and When to Gather

The leaves can be gathered in early spring for tea, and the berries can be gathered by the bucketful in the mid- to late summer. If you harvest the root, wait until fall when the plant begins to die back after harvest.

How to Gather

In the early spring, before the blackberry goes to bloom, gather leaves using a pair of scissors and carefully (being mindful of the thorns) clip off the leaf clusters and then dry them for tea. Take a few pails along on your trail walks in late summer to gather the blackberry fruit. If harvesting the root, use a shovel and clippers. The root is quite spindly, so a considerable amount of root is needed. Wash, chop, and dry for tea.

How to Eat

Blackberry leaves are high in calcium, potassium, iron, zinc, and phosphorus as well as vitamins A, C, E, and B. You can extract these nutrients by boiling the leaves for 20 minutes and enjoy them in a strong hot or iced tea. It mixes well in a tea of red clover, nettle, and oat straw for a mineral-rich drink. If the drink is too "earthy," add ice, and the mineral flavor mellows a bit. Aromatics like spicebush or the barks of aspen, tulip poplar, or birch can be added to spice up the tea, if preferred.

The dark berry, jammy flavor of blackberry is delicious in a variety of desserts, snacks, and preserves, including jam, chutney, and syrups for cocktails and sodas.

Harvesting blackberries growing in a large stand along a route to the lakeshore in August.

Its dark flavor holds up well with tomato ketchup and chili spice flavors, and it can add a nice fruit layer in a smoky habanero sauce for meats and sandwiches.

Future Harvests

Blackberry spreads easily by runners, and the forager can encourage this process by cultivating runners in the immediate area to grow the stand. Though Himalayan blackberry has become invasive in parts of the Pacific Northwest, blackberry is not yet a problem in the Midwest. Wildlife enjoy the fruit, too, and this should be a harvesting consideration, but simply gathering the berries shouldn't significantly impact the stand. Because the plant grows prolifically, harvesting a few roots also shouldn't impact sustainability, but if there is a concern, leaves can be used in the place of the root for an astringent tea.

black cherry

Prunus serotina

EDIBLE fruit, bark

The black cherry offers delightful late summer fruits for foraging. Its tart and slightly savory fruit can be turned into an easy fruit staple in the pantry for baking into pies and fruit leathers and for making healthful beverages.

How to Identify

Black cherry, which can grow upward of 100 feet, is widespread across the Midwest and can be found in mixed hardwood forests alongside the maples and beeches. The bark of a young black cherry is a steely dark gray, nearly black and scored with horizontal lenticels. As the tree matures, the bark becomes rough and shaggy in appearance in a way that is often characterized as "burned potato-chip-like."

The leaves are dark green. They have a shiny topside, and underneath there may be a slightly hairy midrib near the leaf's stem. The leaves are narrow and alternate, simple, and lanceolate with serrated edges.

The white flowers of the black cherry bloom in late spring and grow in long

Black cherry leaves and tiny flower buds, ready to open in early spring.

Black cherry fruits hang from the tree, ready for picking.

racemes. Fruits are smaller than the cultivated cherry and appear in late summer in clusters of up to two dozen small, pea-sized cherries.

Where and When to Gather

The fruit of the black cherry is significantly different than that of the cultivated sweet cherry common in the fruit belt of the Midwest. The fruits are smaller and more tart in flavor. Look for ripe berries in the late summer. If you choose to harvest the young tips of the branches and inner bark to dry for tea, do so when the sap runs in the spring.

How to Gather

Gather young twigs for a plant extract of the cherry bark. In late summer, look for the darkest purple berries and taste them before gathering the clusters. The variability in tartness of the berries (a function of both soil and season) warrants tasting a sample from a particular tree before investing significant time in harvesting. That doesn't mean even the most sour and bitter berry would be inedible; rather, know the flavor profile of that batch and have a use for them in mind as you go along. And harvest in sunny, dry, and hot weather as that naturally increases the sugars available in the fruit. Separate the cherries from the stems and use immediately or freeze for later use.

How to Eat

The young branch tips can be used to make a bitter almond–flavored extract that can

Black cherry bark is sometimes described as looking like burned potato chips.

be used in baking projects that call for almond extract. The spicy bitter flavor can also be used as a staple for cocktails and mixed drinks.

The tart black cherry fruits can be a darling in the summer kitchen for mixed berry pies, crumbles, fruit leathers, and jams. Freeze the abundance for winter's use, or dry them (pitted) for use in baking, morning porridge, and trail mix.

The fruit can also be prepared as a cherry juice concentrate similar to the commercial concentrate made from cultivated cherries, but at a fraction of the cost. Simply cover the crushed berries (stones and all) in water and simmer into a rich concentrate that can be strained off and bottled (or frozen) for later use. The concentrate is high in antioxidants and has anti-inflammatory powers, making the drink a local "superfood." This wild version of cherry juice concentrate can easily replace the commercial variety that is now popular among athletes as a sports recovery drink.

Future Harvests
The black cherry is widespread in mixed hardwood forests across the Midwest. Sustainable bark harvesting practices should be used to prevent the unnecessary destruction of a mature tree. Lower hanging berries are abundant, which means there is always fruit aplenty for local wildlife on higher branches.

black locust

Robinia pseudoacacia

EDIBLE flowers

In mid-spring, the aromatic white clusters of the black locust flower release a jasmine-sweet fragrance on the breeze. It attracts the honeybee for its nectar, but also the forager who gathers the blossoms for an aromatic cocktail syrup, a crunchy addition to a spring salad or chilled soup, or delicious fritters.

How to Identify

Black locust is a tree native to North America, abundant across the Midwest. A tall, sprawling tree, it towers out at 80 feet with a draping canopy of leaves. From a distance the dark, craggy bark resembles that of a shagbark hickory. But looking closely, you'll find compound leaves that have an arrangement of up to 15 small, oval leaflets about 3 inches long and half that across. The black locust blooms in mid- to late spring for about two weeks, with

Fragrant black locust flower clusters ready to harvest.

heavy edible racemes of fragrant, drooping, creamy white flowers. The flowers give
way to pods in the late summer that are 3
inches in length.

Where and When to Gather

Black locust blooms mid- to late spring
for about a two-week period. Listen for
the bees in the trees—they will tell you
when the blossoms are at their most fragrant peak.

How to Gather

Being mindful of the bees gathering the
nectar, gather the racemes of flowers by
simply clipping them from the trees into
large harvest baskets, taking care not to
crush the flowers. The fresh flowers can be
kept in the refrigerator for a few days.

How to Eat

The fresh flavor of the black locust blossom is similar to that of a fresh snap pea.
It is a versatile flavor: they make a beautiful addition to a spring greens salad.

The fresh, green, and crunchy taste pairs
well with tender spring mints and onions,
tossed in vinaigrette as a simple salad.
They also make for a nice addition to a
Vietnamese spring roll. Puree a handful of
the blossoms along with the new shoots
of cattail with yogurt and fresh mint for a
chilled spring yogurt soup and serve it as
an appetizer to a nice light, white fish or
scallops main course.

The blossoms also withstand cooking
and are classically prepared as a fritter,
fried in butter or olive oil. The fragrance
of the flower lends itself to a simple syrup
that works well in mixed drinks, and the
blossoms can also be prepared as a fragrant
jelly.

Future Harvests

The black locust is abundant across the
Midwest and is deemed by some to be
weedy, particularly in disturbed areas.
Gathering the blossoms for personal
household cooking projects will not significantly threaten the plant's sustainability.

black walnut

Juglans nigra

EDIBLE nuts

The grocery-store-variety walnut has nothing on the rich, aromatic flavor of the native wild walnut, found in abundance across the Midwest in late summer and early fall. You will have to endure the tedious effort of gathering, hulling, and shelling to enjoy the decadent nutmeats, but it is well worth the effort.

How to Identify

Towering walnut trees are abundant and native to the Midwest region. When mature, the trees can reach a height of 150 feet, but most are within 80 to 100 feet tall, with trunks 2 to 3 feet in diameter.

The walnut prefers full sun and often grows along the edges of the forest to gain maximum sunlight. The bark is a deeply furrowed gray-black. The compound leaves have up to 23 stemless oval and smooth leaflets.

In midsummer, look for a windfall of walnuts on the sidewalk and streets. But beware: they may look green, but black walnuts stain the pavement, your hands, and anything else they touch. Wear old clothes and gloves while processing.

Walnuts ripening on the tree in summer alongside distinctive compound leaves.

Where and When to Gather

The walnut flowers in late spring and bears globular fruit that fully ripens in late summer, although the windfall of falling walnuts becomes noticeable in midsummer as the green fruits of the black walnut begin to drop. Your main competition for this fruit will be the local wildlife, particularly the ever-aggressive squirrel.

How to Gather

While ultimately you want hulled walnuts to process into dry nuts, be the squirrel by gathering even the green, unhulled nuts, and let them ripen in a bucket. Don't be surprised if there are some worms in the blackening hulls—they are hull maggots

and do not penetrate the walnut's shell.

To process the walnut, you will first have to hull it. Soft, blackened hulls are the easiest to process. Set aside the green hull nuts and wait to process them when they darken. Be sure to wear rubber or leather gloves when handling the blackened hulled walnut, as the nut will permanently stain everything it touches (which means the black walnut can also effectively be used as a fabric dye). Use a hammer to mash the hull, followed by a stiff brush to scrub away the softened, blackened hull, then wash with water. Soaking the nut helps with the hull removal a bit.

After removal of the hull, dry the walnut completely. In low-humidity regions, this can be done on the counter, although a low-heat oven (I prefer the proof setting, or at the most 180 degrees F, to avoid roasting) or a dehydrator can also be used.

When the nuts are completely dry, they need to be shelled. This is a two-part process. First, place the nut inside old rags (to prevent shell shrapnel) and smash it. Pick out the most accessible bits of nutmeat, but add the shell remainders to a bucket for sorting. The second step is sorting out shell bits and picking out any remaining nutmeat from the shell.

In bumper crop years, when the processing may be too much to accomplish by hand in front of a good movie, or even by a group work party, there are many local nut processors across the Midwest who—for a small fee—will hull and shell the nuts for you.

How to Eat

The reward of the tedium of walnut processing comes in the form of a rich, highly aromatic nut that cannot be rivaled in supermarket products. It smells slightly toasted and has tannic and bitter flavors that are more pronounced than in the cultivated walnut. A little goes a long way in the kitchen because of its flavor profile.

The wild walnut shines in baked goods and is delicious atop a steaming hot wild porridge with local maple syrup. The alcohol extract of the slightly crushed walnut hulls can serve as a rich, aromatic baking extract that can be used in the place of commercial almond or vanilla extract, as well as serve as a cocktail-cart staple for flavoring mixed drinks.

And for the cocktail cart, the green hulled walnut can be transformed into a traditional Italian digestif known as nocino, an aromatic spicy liqueur that contains clove, orange peel, nutmeg, and cinnamon. Try making a nocino with the herbs of the spicebush, tulip poplar, and wild ginger. Delish!

Future Harvests

The black walnut is abundant across the Midwest and is deemed by some to even be invasive. Gathering the nuts for household cooking projects will have no impact on the plant's sustainability.

blueberry

Vaccinium species

EDIBLE berries

Wild blueberries are some of the most delicious berries to harvest in the summer. Head out for a hunt with basket and picnic in hand, and your forage could possibly count among the highlights of your summer adventures.

How to Identify

Blueberries grow in colonies. Species vary in height, ranging from small 6- to 8-inch ground cover in the woods to a towering, deciduous shrub of more than 10 feet in open fields and bogs. All berries in the genus *Vaccinium* are edible and inter-changeable in use. The bark of the blue-berry is mostly gray and can sometimes have a bit of green or even pink along the woody stems. The leaves vary in size, but are 1 to 2 inches long, ovate, and simple, with smooth to slightly toothed edges. The whitish pink flowers bloom in late spring and give way to the delicious fruits that ripen in mid- to late summer.

Berries are blue to nearly black and can range in size from ¼ to ¾ inch in

Fruit ready for the eating.

Small wild blueberry plants dot the woodland floor.

diameter, borne singly or in small clusters. The berry's sweetness is both species and season dependent. Smaller berries have a tendency to be more sour than the large varieties, and weather has an effect on the plumpness of the berry.

Where and When to Gather

The wild blueberry harvest peaks in August. Seek out wild blueberries in bogs and in sunny open fields. You'll also find them in the shade as ground cover in mixed hardwood forests and in higher elevations as you exit the Midwestern plains states. When you discover a wild blueberry stand, be ready for an abundance of picking.

How to Gather

Take a bucket and mosquito protection as you head out to gather. Picking berries by hand will guarantee a cleaner pick than with a harvest rake, which will also invariably pull in unwanted twigs, bugs, debris, and undesirable fruit. Time saved in the field with the rake is lost to sorting in the kitchen. Choose fruit that is free of bug damage, blight, or powdery mildew.

How to Eat

Think of all the ways blueberries are enjoyed. Turn the wild fruit into fruit leathers, make pies, dry the berries whole for winter snacking, sprinkle them on porridge or oatmeal, make a crumble, create a compote, or cook up a jam or cocktail syrup.

Future Harvests

Most stands of blueberries offer an abundance of fruit, but of course, always leave some for wildlife. Be mindful to not trample lower ground-covering plants. Habitat loss affects many areas where the wild blueberry grows, so to help preserve these species, consider becoming active in ecosystem restoration and habitat preservation activities.

burdock

Arctium species

gobo

`EDIBLE` roots, stalks, shoots, leaves, seeds

Cursed by farmers, gardeners, and municipal park staff, burdock's virtue is rarely celebrated in the United States, but it is a popular vegetable across the world. Called gobo in Asian grocery stores and sometimes found in popular health food stores and co-ops, burdock is an invaluable and versatile wild food that provides both nutritious greens and roots in abundance for the forager's kitchen.

Burdock stalks can be cut from a plant of this size, peeled, then cooked into stir-fries and sautés.

Burdock flowers in early summer.

How to Identify

Burdock is a hearty biennial plant that thrives in many conditions. It is not at all fazed by poor rocky soil or drought. It loves the disturbed edges of fields and waste sites and is prolific in spreading its seeds. In its first year, burdock is identifiable by its fuzzy basal leaves that grow to about 18 inches long and resemble those of rhubarb. In the second year, burdock sends up a sturdy stalk that goes to flower in midsummer. The flower changes to its famous bur-laden seed casing, each of which contain several hundred small seeds in late fall.

Where and When to Gather

While burdock is found virtually everywhere across the Midwest, take care in selecting a harvest area with softer, rich, well-drained soil. Because burdock grows abundantly in urban and scrub areas, be sure it is free of herbicidal applications, lead, or environmental pollutants. A great way to identify a clean spot for harvesting is to contact a local organic farmer in your area; chances are she has burdock on her land and is more than happy to allow you to do some digging (just remember to backfill your holes).

Burdock is known for its nutritious yet sturdy taproot that affixes the plant

Burdock grows enthusiastically and is considered invasive by some. Enjoy in abundance its root and shoots.

solidly to the ground. The first-year roots are easiest to gather for this reason, but second-year roots are equally edible (although potentially woody). The tender small greens of the first-year plant can also be gathered, as can the stalk of a second-year plant before the burdock goes to flower.

How to Gather

Bring a spade to dig out the burdock root. Be prepared for some serious digging, especially if the plants are in the second year, as the taproot can have quite the underground footprint. Dig in a wide circumference so as not to shear off the taproot. Also be prepared to scrub the root in the kitchen, as wild burdock is much more gnarled than its cultured gobo counterpart, and small pockets can retain a significant amount of soil. Use the cleaned root for cooking. To prepare for a tea, chop the clean root into small pieces, dry completely in a dehydrator, and store in an airtight container.

Harvest small, basal leaves in the spring of the plant's first or second year (before it sends up stalks). The stalk and shoots of the second-year plant can be trimmed with pruners, but only until the plant goes to flower, at which point the stalk becomes very woody and inedible.

How to Eat

From root to seed, burdock is completely edible and highly nutritious. Burdock root is a mildly sweet, nourishing carbohydrate. It is a versatile starchy vegetable that can be eaten raw julienned in salads, or it can be mashed, roasted, and even pickled. The young, tender greens are high in vitamins and minerals such as iron, magnesium, and calcium. They can be sautéed, included in a stir-fry, or added to soups. If you are cooking the stems, peel as you would a fibrous rhubarb stalk and then julienne it for salads or stir-fry. The dehydrated root can be toasted and roasted in an iron skillet and then combined in herbal tea blends with roasted chicory root, dandelion root, calendula, and spearmint for an earthy root tea.

Future Harvests

Burdock is considered a noxious weed by many, but maybe if we relearn its virtues, focus will shift to the value of the plant. Currently, however, burdock is subject to aggressive plant management strategies by gardeners, farmers, and park staff. There's a partnership opportunity waiting to grow between the foragers and these land stewards who wish to more sustainably manage the growth and use of this plant, but currently there is little concern for overharvesting.

catnip

Nepeta cataria

catmint

leaves, flowers

Catnip is an aromatic mint with a distinctly musky aroma. It can be used as a culinary herb to add aromatic notes to cocktails, as a culinary flavoring agent in baked goods, and as a soothing and refreshing tea.

How to Identify

Catnip is a clumping, dusty green, mint family plant. It stands about 2 to 3 feet tall with soft and downy heart-shaped leaves oppositely arranged on its square stems. The plant is small and tender through midsummer, when it sends up its flower stalks with blossoms that range in color from white to pinkish and even a deep purple (especially the garden breeds and species escaped from cultivation).

Catnip leaves are most tender and fragrant in the spring.

Where and When to Gather

Catnip is a rough-and-tumble plant—it doesn't mind scrubby, nutrient-depleted soil, and is easily found in vacant lands in the city. Catnip is also found along the edges of the grassy fields and hedgerows of parks, gardens, and farms. Gather stalks in early summer, before the plant blooms.

How to Gather

Gather and bundle the full stalks and dry for tea. To preserve the aromatics, cut down the leaves and stalks of the plant when fully dry and store in airtight containers.

How to Eat

A plant extract of catnip is useful in blending cocktails, as it melds well with a dark rum, Brazilian cachaca, or peaty scotch. Its earthy and bitter flavors provide excellent base notes blended with cocktail bitters, and the extract can mix well with foraged desert sage, wild ginger, burdock root, and tulip poplar. It's an excellent addition to a forager's Negroni.

If you make a simple syrup, choose a brown sugar which will bring out the deep musky flavors. The syrup can be used to make toffee or flavor a pistachio or caramel ice cream. Catnip is a useful herb to have in your tea cabinet as it's very relaxing and soothing. To minimize any bitter flavors, it's best as a tea made with cool water and served over ice with lemon. Add a sprig of lavender and a dollop of raw honey.

Catnip flowers in early summer. The flowers can also be gathered for tea.

Future Harvests

Catnip is a common wild plant and considered by many a weedy one. As a perennial, the catnip you identify this season will be there next season provided you haven't harvested the entire plant lock, stock, and barrel. Therefore, harvest the above-ground parts of the plant in moderation. If you would like to grow a stand of catnip, it can be propagated with cuttings from the parent plant.

cattail

Typha angustifolia, *T. latifolia*, and other species

EDIBLE rhizome, shoots, spikes, pollen

Growing in thick stands in wetlands and marshes, cattail is a perfect food for the forager as it offers a starchy rhizome, delicious and edible green shoots, and a protein-rich pollen useful in flour mixes and vegetable dishes.

How to Identify

The common cattail is found in areas of full sun in knee-deep water, where gravel or rock lines the bottom of the wetland. Its solid stalk reaches heights of nearly 10 feet and has long, erect basal leaves that are often described as swordlike on each side of the stalk. Both male and female parts (spikes) exist on the same plant, and the male spike forms pollen in midsummer.

Where and When Gather

Beginning in early spring, young shoots off the rhizome can be harvested and boiled

Cattails, shown here in spring, are abundant in wetland areas. Choose a locale away from wetland pollution and traffic to do your harvesting.

Pollen is found on the male spike in early summer. Gather the pollen on a dry, windless day by tapping it into a paper bag.

like asparagus or sautéed similarly. The new stalk can also be prepared and used as a cooked green before it goes to flower.

The male spike is edible in spring, blanched and served as a crunchy green vegetable, with a texture similar to corn. In early summer, the male spike will produce a yellow, protein-rich pollen (my favorite). In the fall, the cattail rhizome offers you a nutritious starch.

Take note that other plants—particularly calamus and iris—grow in similar environs as the common cattail, but do not reach the heights of the cattail or feature characteristics like the flowering spikes. Proper and careful identification of cattail and calamus, which have a delicious, aromatic root, will help avoid any confusion with iris, whose inedible root will cause sickness. Also, harvest from wetland areas that are free from environmental runoff or are upstream from pollution sources.

How to Gather
Using a sharp knife, cut the young shoots off the rhizome. Snap off the male spikes

with pruners, being sure to leave some spikes to pollinate the cattails later in the summer.

Carefully gather pollen from the male spike in early summer, on a calm day without wind, into a closed container to prevent it from blowing away. Store in a paper bag in the refrigerator until ready to use.

Processing the starch collected from the rhizome in fall is a tedious process, but worth experimenting with once or twice to develop a sense of how to do it efficiently. In the fall after the plant has begun to die back, select a spot along the shore in clear water (you do not want a muddy harvest). Using a sharp knife, make cuttings 4 to 6 inches long from the rhizome between the stalks (for easy handling) and deposit them in a clean container.

In the kitchen, peel back the rind of the rhizome to expose the starchy interior core. Submerge the cuttings in water and briskly scrub the pieces together to help extract the starch from the rhizome. Once the starch settles to the bottom, strain off the water and store the starch in a glass jar. The starch liquid can be frozen in small batches.

How to Eat

The early season shoots, spikes, and young stalks are all delicious in various stir-fries, sautés, and roasted with butters and olive oils (but only before these parts get too woody or mature later in the growing season). These cooked greens have a nourishing sweet flavor similar to bamboo shoots or sweet corn. The male spikes particularly have an earthy sweet-corn note when boiled and eaten off the main stalk (you can eat the stalk, too, depending on tenderness).

The protein-rich plant pollen collected from the fruiting male spike can be sifted and incorporated into a flour mix, stirred into porridge and vegetable dishes, or added to a smoothie for anyone who prefers to add or increase plant-based protein in their diets. The dehydrated or liquefied starch made from the rhizome can be used to thicken soups and stews, and also can be incorporated into baking projects that require a thickener.

Future Harvests

The wetland environment in which the cattail thrives is constantly under barrage by development and environmental runoff and watershed pollution. This affects not only the plant's future growth, but also its edibility. The cattail can be a future sustainable food as long as we are good stewards and work together to protect our wetlands and watersheds.

chaga

Inonotus obliquus

EDIBLE fruiting body

Chaga is relatively easy to identify, and is a safe and versatile foraged mushroom that is fun and delicious to experiment with in the kitchen. With a flavor of chocolate earthiness, chaga works well in teas, baked goods, dark microbrews, and even skin products.

Chaga harvest ready for processing. Look for its burl-like shape on dying birch trees.

How to Identify

With experience, you will be able to recognize chaga on the bark of a dying birch tree. What looks like a burl on the birch is actually a gnarled expression of the fruit of the fungus, with a dark black, craggy exterior layer and reddish interior. Chaga is a hard, woody parasitic fungus that grows out of the wounds of birch trees. It grows across the Northern Hemisphere in forests and can be found across the Midwest where birch trees are plentiful.

Where and When to Gather

Gather chaga that is of a reasonable size (at least 4 to 6 inches in diameter), taking care to leave a portion of the fruiting body attached to the tree. It can be gathered all year.

How to Gather

Bring along a mallet or small hammer, hand axe, or small hacksaw to remove the chaga from the tree. It is very sturdy material. Be sure to remove only the external fruiting body (growing above the bark) so the inner fruiting body can continue to digest the decaying birch tree and regrow chaga.

In the kitchen, chaga is nearly impossible to process without the use of heavy stone tools, a hammer, and a wood rasp to grind it down to a beautifully fine powder for infusions. Do not put whole chaga pieces in your blender or spice grinder: they will most likely burn out your motor and ruin your blade. Instead, use a wood rasp to grate the chaga. Some say to remove the blackened exterior shell of the mushroom, but I just use the whole thing. You might want to wear protective eyewear, too, lest you find chunks of flying chaga in your eyeball.

How to Eat

Rich in antioxidants and polysaccharides, chaga has a deliciously rich aroma and flavor profile of dark chocolate. The ground or powdered chaga can be added directly to a tomato-based sauce, chili, or chocolate and peanut butter-based dessert or smoothie (think of adding chaga to a chocolate flourless cake or black bean brownie). The polysaccharides of chaga are best extracted in a long simmering decoction in water, which can then be drunk as a tea.

Chaga is delicious added to boiled stovetop coffee or a wild-foraged chai, adding deep chocolate notes to the brew. Local brewmasters are also starting to add chaga to brews of porters and stouts, as it adds that chocolate flavor and pairs well with other flavoring agents such as hops without adding an overly flavored aspect to the brew.

Future Harvests

Because chaga is becoming popular and has been qualified as a locavore's "superfood," sustainable and careful harvesting of chaga is recommended. Be mindful of your harvesting techniques so as not to remove the entire fruiting body from the tree, and chaga will continue to grow.

chestnut

Castanea species

`EDIBLE` nut

The chestnut is an amazing food, filled with protein, minerals, vitamins, and carbohydrate energy. It's a complete food and also versatile in the kitchen with its neutral and approachable flavor that everyone will enjoy baked into breads, soups, casseroles, and even roasted over an open fire.

How to Identify

The true American chestnut is virtually extinct from North American forests because of a 20th-century fungal blight that wiped the tree from the landscape. What foragers will find escaped from cultivation in the woods and in landscaping are American-Chinese-Euro hybrids, which exhibit traits similar to those of the American chestnut, including the versatile, delicious, and nutritious edible nut.

Most chestnut species reach heights of only 20 to 30 feet. The bark is dark gray and deeply furrowed, with flat-topped

Fallen nuts ready for gathering.

Chestnuts in the husk on the tree in the fall.

ridges. The shiny, toothed-edged green leaves are 5 to 9 inches long, oblong, and ending in a point. Chestnut flowers in late spring and then produces a very spiny bur that ripens in fall with three or four chestnut fruits inside.

Don't confuse *Castanea* species with the horse chestnut, *Aesculus hippocastanum*, which also produces a spiny bur about the same time as the chestnut. The horse chestnut is inedible and used only in herbal medicine.

Where and When to Gather

You can find the tree growing along the edges of mixed hardwood forests, in areas with well-drained soil and sunshine. If you cannot locate trees on your own, frequently local-food resources can also help you connect to a local chestnut grower who may allow gleaning of the excess fallen nuts.

The spiny burs of the tree split open and fall to the ground in late September. A ripe bur will detach easily from the tree and contain two or three well-formed chestnuts. The chestnuts inside will be fleshy, shiny, chocolate-brown in color, and firm to the touch. It is a brief harvest season, about two weeks.

How to Gather

Because the bur of the chestnut is extremely spiny, leather gloves are required for gathering and handling. A nut gatherer is highly recommended and fun for harvesting, especially with small children. Carefully extract the nut from the bur, and store the nuts themselves in a cold storage area (refrigerator, basement, or cold storage) or freezer until processing to prevent sprouting. Discard or compost any nuts that mildew or sprout.

How to Eat

For an easy appetizer that kids will enjoy, roast the chestnuts on the stovetop, but first score a slit with a sharp knife in the bottom of the shell to allow the moisture to escape (thus eliminating exploding chestnuts). Once roasted, they can be easily peeled and enjoyed warm from the shell. They have a very neutral, buttery flavor, making them an especially easy food for children to both prepare and appreciate.

French, Spanish, eastern European, and Asian cooking traditions include the chestnut as a traditional food. It can be pickled, pureed into soups, and turned into delectable desserts like the classic Mont Blanc.

Future Harvests

The window to harvest chestnuts is small and the competition with wildlife relatively fierce. Given the limited distribution of wild chestnut trees, a big consideration for the forager is in helping re-establish the tree in mixed hardwood forests. Partnering with growers to make plantings of hybrid varieties on fungus-resistant rootstock can help.

CAUTION Horse chestnuts (*Aesculus hippocastanum*) are often confused for chestnuts but are inedible and used only in herbal medicine.

chickweed

Stellaria media

`EDIBLE` stem, leaves, flowers

For most gardeners and farmers, chickweed is an early spring, self-sowing, bothersome weed. Chickweed tastes markedly bright and green, similar to the flavor of wheatgrass, but is moist, succulent, slightly crunchy, and more substantial.

How to Identify

Chickweed is a bright green, low-growing, mat-forming spring annual that reaches a maximum height of about 12 inches. Chickweed loves nutrient-rich, well-draining soil. It has small opposite leaves with slender stems, and its late spring flowers are white and have five deeply notched petals. Hold a cutting of chickweed up to the light, and you will notice its chief (and fun) identifier: there is a single line of hair that runs on the side of the stem. To better

Tender chickweed loves cool, moist weather and is most vibrant and ready for harvest in the height of spring.

notice the fine hairs, use a magnifying glass or hand-held loupe.

Where and When to Gather

Chickweed is a low-growing, creeping green that can be found along edges of the trail in rich soil in mid- to late spring. Very commonly, it is found in the well-composted fields of farms and gardens. Chickweed loves cool, moist weather, and is most vibrant and ready for harvest in the height of spring (May), In mid-June, it begins to die back after it has gone to flower. Chickweed returns in late fall when the rains and cooler weather come in, though that wave normally is not as vibrant as the spring crop.

How to Gather

Chickweed can be harvested easily with kitchen shears in the field—the stem, leaf, and flowers are all edible. Take care to harvest only clean plant material, as chickweed can easily gather dust and debris or mud as it grows along the ground, and I find it difficult to completely clean in the kitchen.

How to Eat

Chickweed shines as a raw, green vegetable. Cooking chickweed changes the flavor tremendously, from bright, grassy green to a more swampy cooked flavor, particularly if you are cooking the plant in an oil or butter. Some don't mind the plant cooked down, but there are other greens that shine as cooked greens in the spring, like nettle or garlic mustard.

Chickweed can be eaten raw, chopped into salads, or used in dishes that call for bean sprouts—think Vietnamese spring rolls or pad thai. It is delicious as a great addition to a green smoothie recipe and can be juiced like wheatgrass in a masticating juicer. Chickweed can be blended to add volume to a foraged spring pesto, and it can help temper the strong flavor of a springtime garlic mustard pesto.

Future Harvests

Chickweed self-sows abundantly, and harvesting its leaves and flowers won't harm its ability to reproduce significantly. In fact, if you decide to plant chickweed in your garden, do so with care as it can take over very quickly.

chicory

Cichorium intybus

`EDIBLE` leaves, roots

Chicory is a delicious wild relative to cultivated endives (bitter greens) popular in European culinary traditions. In spring, the young, tender leaves of chicory dot the thawing landscape alongside dandelion, dock, and wild lettuce, a perfect addition to a salad or wild spring greens frittata.

How to Identify

Chicory is widespread across the Midwest. In early spring, the perennial chicory is a basal rosette of long, pinnately lobed leaves with a large midrib vein. In the height of summer, the mature flowering chicory can tower well over 6 feet. Its sprawling stalks extend wildly in every direction, decorated with beautiful blue flowers. The flat-tipped flowers range in color from cornflower blue to translucent blue purple and range from ½ inch to 2 inches across. The long, whitish taproot is similar to that of dandelion, and the root and stem contain a milky sap.

Where and When to Gather

Chicory is found in open fields and empty lots and along roadways. It frequently is interspersed with dandelion, dock, and Queen Anne's lace. In the early spring, you will want to harvest the tender leaves for salads. In later summer and into fall, gather the roots. As chicory likes rocky, gravely, and dry soil, it is sometimes difficult to remove the root in its entirety.

How to Gather

Harvest in the early morning when the leaves are more sweet than bitter, and choose to gather smaller leaves. To gather roots in the fall, choose a spot in soil that is less rocky and damp to make harvesting easier. Clean, chop, and dry the root in a dehydrator, then store in an airtight container for later use.

How to Eat

The tender spring leaves can be gathered and eaten in salads along with other early spring greens. Bitter plays an important role in digestion and metabolism of foods—don't shy away from the flavor and the foods that offer it.

The leaves of the mature chicory also remain edible, though by midsummer they are significantly more tough, dry, and bitter than the tender leaves of spring. These larger leaves can be stir-fried with other greens, or eaten fresh and massaged with a nice mustard vinaigrette.

Chicory root is a bit rough and spindly

The friendly blue of the chicory flower in summer identifies this delicious perennial green.

to be used as a roasted or cooked root vegetable, but it can be harvested, dried, and roasted to make a tea. Chicory is a great addition to a foraged herbal chai tea, blended with the likes of dandelion root, burdock root, sassafras root, chaga, spicebush berry, and a black tea. The roasted chicory root tea has a pleasant earthy flavor and certainly can stand on its own as a unique beverage. However, while it may be referred to as the poor man's coffee, it really is not a substitute for *Coffea arabica*!

Future Harvests

Chicory is widely distributed across the Midwest and self sows easily, making it an excellent choice for your harvest.

cleavers

Galium aparine

EDIBLE leaves, stems

Seek out leggy cleavers, spreading across the forest floor in early spring, for a nourishing "spring cleaning" food. It has a green flavor similar to wheatgrass and is high in vitamin C.

Small, whorled shoots of cleavers appear in early spring. They soon grow leggy and tall, but can still be used for tea, or use the plant in recipes as you would wheatgrass.

How to Identify

Cleavers is a sprawling plant, with leggy, square stems that have eight-leaved whorls that run along the stems. In mid-spring, it produces petite four-petaled white flowers that bear fuzzy, lobed fruit the size of a small pea. The plant clings easily to both people and pets on woodland walks.

Where and When to Gather

In the early spring, the whorls of cleavers spring from the ground and begin to sprawl across the ground and over low foliage in wooded areas with rich, damp soil. Look for cleavers in the shady edges of the woods.

How to Gather

Gather the tender whorls as they emerge from the ground in early spring until they start to go to seed in late spring and die back. Cleavers can be picked by hand or with kitchen scissors. You will find they easily pull completely out of the ground: the roots aren't firmly attached to the ground and usually dislodge easily, and the whole plant can be used at that point. Try to harvest as little dirt as possible, because cleavers are somewhat difficult to clean.

How to Eat

Cleavers have a bright green flavor, but the very dry and rough texture, especially as the plant matures, makes it unsuitable for basic salad greens. Because cleavers are full of chlorophyll and vitamin C, they are a good addition to a green smoothie recipe, or juice the leaves like wheatgrass. Shots of juiced cleavers can be frozen in ice cube trays for later use in blender drinks. Thousands of tiny hooked hairs on the stems and leaves can cling to your mouth and throat, so cooking, blending, or juicing are preferable ways to prepare them for food or beverages.

Future Harvests

Cleavers grow abundantly in the springtime and are vigorous in their ability to self-seed. Gathering the plant even in abundance won't significantly impact the plant's sustainability.

cow parsnip

Heracleum maximum

EDIBLE leaves, stems, seeds, roots

From spring until midsummer, the common cow parsnip grows abundantly and offers its leaves, stems, and seeds as foods that can be used in stir-fries, soups, and egg dishes, or paired with strong-flavored cheeses.

Cow parsnip in flower in midsummer.

How to Identify

Cow parsnip is widely distributed across the Midwest, particularly in open fields and along stream beds. It is somewhat shade tolerant and frequently borders the edges of the woodland. It prefers wet, damp soil.

Cow parsnip emerges from the soil in early spring, with 3- to 5-inch, maple leaf-shaped leaves that that unfurl into leaflets more than a foot in length. The leaf stalks are notably swollen and are arranged alternately along a tall, hollow green stem that will grow as tall as 5 feet. The stem should not have any indications of purple or spotting, as this is a characteristic for both angelica, which is edible, and poison hemlock, which is poisonous. (See angelica for more details and photos differentiating these plants.)

The blossoms of cow parsnip unfurl in the early summer into large, flat, and compound umbels with white flower clusters as large as a foot across. The long, oblong seeds are ready for gathering by late summer. The root is spindly and creamy white; it tastes like a garden parsnip.

Where and When to Gather

Look for cow parsnip in the damp shade of woodlands and ditches. The leaves can be collected in early spring, and the flowers and seeds in mid- to late summer. The roots can be collected in the fall as the plant dies back.

The leaves of cow parsnip are markedly different than those of other Apiaceae family plants. They unfold into large 3- to 5-inch leaves that have a maple leaf-like shape and which then unfurl into leaflets more than a foot in length.

How to Gather

Gather the first tender leaves of cow parsnip in early spring. The stems can be gathered as they begin to grow tall, though they start to become significantly more woody once the plant's umbel unfurls. Gather the seeds when the seed head folds up and the seeds are mostly dry, then finish drying them in a dehydrator and store them for later use. The roots can be gathered with a small shovel once the plant begins to die.

How to Eat

The tender spring leaves and petioles of cow parsnip can be boiled and then used in a multitude of dishes that require cooked greens. They can also be enjoyed simply topped with rich butter, fresh spring herbs

The dry seeds of cow parsnip can be gathered and used as an aromatic culinary spice similar to carrot seed.

root vegetables to create a nicely balanced root mélange that can be enjoyed with spring herbs and onions. The seeds can be fully dried and ground in the kitchen to create an aromatic, celery-carrot-parsnip–like seasoning. Use it in salads, soups, or dressings.

Future Harvests

Cow parsnip is abundant across the Midwest, and in many areas, particularly ranching country, is included on the list of invasive species. Gathering the plant (in areas free of herbicidal applications) for food is actually an opportunity to control its distribution in a sustainable way, in lieu of using chemicals as a plant management strategy.

like wild onion and parsley, and a bit of tamari or soy sauce. The flavors of both the greens and stems are hearty enough to be paired with strongly flavored cheeses and in egg dishes. Cow parsnip works well with heavy French-style cooking, anything with lots of butter, eggs, and cream.

The fresh stems can be cut and sliced into manageable pieces and parboiled, then added to stir-fries or fresh spring soups. Some prefer to peel the stems first, but this can result in an overcooked, mushy stalk, fine for a pureed soup, but not for a stir-fry. The root can be boiled and then roasted. Combine it with other

Caution

Cow parsnip is a perennial in the family Apiaceae, and care in identification is important to not confuse it with poison hemlock, a poisonous relative (see angelica). Learn the chief identifiers between these plants and only harvest if you are 100 percent certain of your identification. Also, cow parsnip contains compounds that, once on your skin and exposed to the sun, may result in a reaction that can range from a rash to a blistering burn for some with especially sensitive skin. Best to be safe: wear gloves while harvesting.

crabapple

Malus species

`EDIBLE` fruit

The crabapple is a wild apple variety that is small, less that 2 inches in diameter. It possesses all the virtuous qualities of the wild apple and is a plentiful foraged fruit. It also is a delicious grab-and-go trail snack for hikers and runners.

How to Identify

Crabapple trees are widely distributed across the Midwest, in fields and hedgerows. In the spring, crabapple trees are filled with clusters of pinkish white to deep rose-colored flowers that attract honeybees.

Like the wild apple, the crabapple tree has brown, scaly bark with dense branches.

Its leaves are ovate and scalloped, with a gray underside. The fruit begins to ripen in summer; a wet growing season will yield 1- to 2-inch fruit ranging from yellow to red.

Where and When to Gather

Look for crabapples to grow in abundance on public land, near hiking trails, in orchards, and on farmsteads. The

Crabapple blossoms are beautiful and showy in mid-spring.

Crabapples on the tree in the fall. Taste your way through the harvest to ensure your crabapples are a bit juicy and have a good balance of tart and sweet flavors.

crabapple is also a common ornamental and often the fruit is left unharvested. Of course, always ask permission before gathering on private property. The fruit is ready in late summer and well into the fall.

How to Gather

The growing season affects the crabapple's flavor. A dry season will result in a drier, more mealy fruit. A wet season will result in a more juicy, succulent fruit. As the fruit ripens, the crabapple becomes more sweet. Wait for the ripening crabapples to soften, and harvest them after the first frost as they will be noticeably more sweet. Choose fruit that has little insect damage or molds.

How to Eat

The crabapple will be more tart than its larger wild apple counterpart, but it is nonetheless of value. The crabapple can be swapped out by equal weight for recipes calling for apples.

Apple butters, chutneys, applesauce, jelly, cider, crumbles, pies, and fruit leathers can all be prepared with the crabapple. Because the fruit is small, removing the seeds can sometimes be tedious. The fruit should first be run through a food mill for recipes like sauces and leathers to improve texture of the final product. Crabapples can be pressed and fermented into raw apple cider vinegars as well as made into ciders.

Future Harvests

The crabapple is common throughout the Midwest, and harvesting its fruit will have little impact on the tree's distribution and growth.

cranberry
Vaccinium oxycoccos
EDIBLE fruit

Of course, when one thinks of cranberries, the traditional holiday cranberry sauce comes to mind. But this late-season fruit isn't just for the holiday table. The wild cranberry is a delicious find, high in antioxidants and vitamins, that can be preserved for year-round enjoyment.

How to Identify

The wild, woody branches of the cranberry can grow up to a foot and spread along the ground over nearby vegetation, creating a mat of cranberry plant from which to harvest. The dark green leaves of the cranberry are small, up to an inch long, and grow with short petioles (the stalk connecting the leaf to the stem). The leaves are rough and ovate, and they alternate along a

Cranberry fruit is a delicious fall foraging find.

long greenish-red stem. The flowers vary in color from whitish to pinkish; they appear singly at the end of a long stalk.

Where and When to Gather

The cranberry is an evergreen vining plant that can spread across rocky outcrops and low-lying brush. It also grows well along sandy lake shores, bogs, and other wet locations.

The flowers set fruit on an 18-month cycle, beginning in June of the first summer when the fruit first sets. The plant then goes dormant until the following summer when the fruit then develops and ripens, ready for harvest in the fall. The berries overwinter well and can even be discovered on winter hikes in areas where the snow has blown away.

How to Gather

The berries can easily be gathered by hand into baskets, and as bogs are amazing places, you should make an adventure of the day, packing in a picnic to enjoy the experience. The smaller of the cranberry varieties are more tedious to pick by hand, but worth the effort as it is a berry high in nutrient content and it stores well.

If the vines are clear of other vegetation, a hand rake used for wild blueberry picking can work well for gathering and decreasing picking time, but its use will also gather unwanted leaves and plant material that will need to be removed later.

How to Eat

The cranberry is a classic fall and holiday staple that is full of flavor. The fruits are high in antioxidants, making it a good local "superfood." Firm, clean, and dry cranberries can be stored for many months in dry cloth market bags in the bottom of the refrigerator or cold storage through the winter. The cranberries can also be dried in a dehydrator for baking, porridge, and snacking. In addition to simmering a cranberry chutney or sauce with the berries, you can make a juice or simple syrup, both of which are delicious in kitchen and cocktail projects.

Future Harvests

The biggest threat to the wild cranberry isn't over-harvesting, but rather the rapid rate at which wetland and bogland is disappearing to development across the upper Midwest, as well as upstream watershed pollution and contamination. The bog is a magical place, and each forager should give back in ways to help protect and preserve this fragile ecosystem.

currant

Ribes species
gooseberry
`EDIBLE` berries

In the height of summer, currants hang off the stem with a sweet juniper-like fragrance. Back in the kitchen, these common berries can be transformed into myriad and delicious baked goods, preserves, and cocktails.

How to Identify

There are well over 70 varieties of *Ribes* across the Midwest and into the mountain states. Generally delineated by having thorns (gooseberries) or not having thorns (currants) along the branches, both are similar in flavor and can be used interchangeably. The leaves are silvery green, free of hair, like a maple leaf in shape, and range from 1½ to 2 inches in size.

The small fruit of *Ribes* species grow singly or in clusters and range in color from a translucent gold to bright red to dark

Currants are harvested for pâte de fruits, fruit leather, and crème de cassis.

Currants on the bush in midsummer have a sweet juniper flavor.

How to Gather

Gather the fruits in the warmth of the day, when the berries will be the most sweet. The fruit will be fragrant, resinous, and slightly sticky, leaving your fingers smelling juniper-sweet.

How to Eat

The currant is such a delight to transform into delicious summer dishes. The berry shines served fresh over soft local cheese. Currants can also be prepared in a variety of preserves, jams, and chutneys, but strain them through a food mill to first remove the seeds. Currants bake well and make delicious mixed berry fruit tarts, breads and muffins, pâte de fruits, and an amazing classic French clafoutis pastry.

On the cocktail cart, crème de cassis is a traditional European liqueur made with the black currant. A foraged variety of crème de cassis can be made by steeping a harvest of mashed black currants in a grain-neutral spirit. Strain the mash and sweeten the juice with raw locally produced honey or maple syrup, and it is ready for use. Currants can also be prepared as a quick simple syrup to complement vodka drinks or to mix with ginger simple syrups and mints.

black, especially those that are escaped wild hybrids. The berries and foliage of the currant are notably resinous, with juniper notes in their fragrance.

Where and When to Gather

Currants and gooseberries are at their full ripeness in the height of summer, late July through early August in most places. Seek them along the edges of the woods and trail, and you might be lucky enough to find the fruit warm in the summer sun.

Future Harvest

Currants and gooseberries reproduce easily in open spaces. You can help propagate stands of currants: cuttings transplant easily.

dandelion

Taraxacum officinale

`EDIBLE` leaves, roots, flowers

For those new to foraging; the dandelion is most certainly one of the first plants to begin foraging. It's usually found right outside the front stoop of the house and offers its leaves, root, and flower—all for delicious use in the kitchen.

Dandelion flowers are a quintessential sign of spring—and of a good meal besides.

Dandelion leaves, which grow in a basal rosette, are toothed and smooth. While it appears hairless on the midrib, if you look through a magnifying lens, you can see soft hairs along the leaf's midvein and on the flower stalk.

How to Identify

The sharply toothed and smooth leaves of the dandelion are some of the spring season's first green edibles. The leaves shoot up from the white crown of the root in a basal rosette first, then several smooth, hollow, 3- to 4-inch flower stalks emerge. Dandelion flowers are familiar—yellow, flat, and cupped by small, pointed bracts that turn upward and close the flower when rain is imminent.

The root's size and girth are dependent on soil: roots are more substantial in well-drained, composted soils and less so in dry, rocky, nutrient-deficient earth.

Where and When to Gather

In early spring, the rapidly growing leaves will be most tender and choice for eating raw when the weather is cool and moist. The leaves are again tender and delicious in cool fall weather. In mid-spring as the weather warms, the flowers can be gathered by hand. The root can be dug anytime across the season.

How to Gather

Harvest the leaves with garden shears or by hand, and clean them gently in the kitchen. The leaves are best picked in the early morning. Plants that are in the shade will be less bitter and more tender and sweet than those in the direct sun. They will also bloom later as well.

Leaves become significantly more bitter, dry, and rough after the dandelion goes to flower and seed and as the weather becomes warm in summer. Flower heads can be plucked from the plant easily with fingers, but they do not wash well, so choose plants that are free from significant dust and debris.

Depending on the soil, the root can be either easy or difficult to remove from the earth. A hand-digging tool can be helpful; take care not to break off the taproot midway. The crowns and root gather significant soil and will require a good brushing and scrubbing in the kitchen.

How to Eat

The dandelion is a nutritionally valuable plant, and once you learn to prepare it in delicious ways, it's easy to get buy-in from others to start harvesting this abundant edible. The tender leaves are best enjoyed in a wild salad of other spring greens with basswood, violet, dock, chicory, wild onion, and wild carrot. If this flavor takes awhile to appreciate, light dressings like a lemon vinaigrette can help offset the bitter. Bitter greens like dandelion help in digestion. It's a good spring habit to add handfuls of wild leaves even into cultivated dishes a few times a day, if possible. Your health will appreciate it.

The root can be roasted, or it can be boiled and combined with other foraged roots for a mash, but dandelion roots are exceptionally good dried, roasted, and added into a foraged tea blend. Roasting sweetens the root and brings out its nutty flavor.

Dandelion leaves and crowns to be cleaned and added to a stir-fry.

Future Harvest

Dandelion's nutrition and versatility in the kitchen, plus its abundance, make it such an outstanding vegetable that it never ceases to amaze me why homeowners everywhere don't just allow the dandelion to take over the green space for cultivation. It truly is a wildly free salad bed.

daylily
Hemerocallis fulva
ditch lily
EDIBLE flowers, shoots, tubers

The wild orange daylily is a common flower found in midsummer across ditches and gullies. *Hemerocallis fulva* is deemed as invasive by gardeners and conservationists, but its flowers, shoots, and tubers are a simply yummy early spring green and summer food for the foraged table.

Daylily stand in the spring.

Harvesting daylily tubers and young shoots.

How to Identify

There are over 60,000 varieties of daylily, and not all are edible. *Hemerocallis fulva* is most chiefly identifiable by its bright orange, six-petaled flower, which can bloom from early July into August, depending on your location within the Midwest. Each bloom lasts only one day. The daylily propagates by a creamy white tuber. Its leaves are smooth, long, and pointed, and the flower stalks are hollow, leafless, and up to 36 inches in length.

Where and When to Gather

The common daylily prefers moist but well-drained soil. It is also found in parks and open spaces, usually without intentional cultivation. It is common in gardens as a low-maintenance landscaping ornamental. Gather the shoots in the early spring as they emerge from the soil. Daylily flowers open up as early as the end of June and can bloom until late July. The tubers can be gathered across the year.

Young daylily shoots unfurling. Each daylily leaf, as it emerges from the shoot, is folded in half lengthwise. Iris leaves are not folded, but flat.

How to Gather

Daylily shoots can be clipped in early spring for cooked greens. In dry weather you can also gather unopened buds with kitchen shears. The blooms open up in the high summer; cut them with kitchen shears for the kitchen. The stalks can also be harvested with kitchen shears and will last several days in the refrigerator. The tubers can be dug anytime—usually with a small shovel—and can be stored for a few weeks in a cold, dry area.

How to Eat

Use the early spring shoots of the daylily as cooked greens for stir-fries and fritta- tas. Edible daylily blooms are delightful to gather and look beautiful atop fresh, green summer salads. The open daylily flowers can be stuffed with a soft cheese and green onion and then fried in butter like stuffed squash blossoms. The unopened buds can also be sautéed in butter with garlic; they have a fresh green taste. The tubers are quite substantial and can be chopped and

sautéed in butter. Their crisp texture also makes them ideal for pickling. The flavor is similar to that of sunchoke pickles.

Future Harvests

With little harm to the overall wild stand's population, the forager can dig an entire plant as the tubers reproduce in abundance. Many gardeners give this plant away for free as they divide the perennial in the fall.

dock

Rumex species

EDIBLE leaves, seeds, root

From the blighted city lots to the vast, open prairie, dock thrives. It's valuable for its nutritious greens, mineral-rich root, and protein-packed seeds.

How to Identify

Perennial dock is easy to identify. The cold-tolerant leaves emerge in early spring with straight, wavy, or curly edges, and they grow from 3 to 12 inches long across the season. Dock puts up tall flower stalks in midsummer, reaching up to 5 feet in height and bearing whorled and small green flowers. These tiny flowers ripen by late summer into thousands of brown, winged seeds. Dock roots are substantial, even larger in nutrient-rich soil, and range in color from creamy white to yellow. The entire plant is predominantly bitter in flavor.

Where and When to Gather

Dock is cold tolerant, so you will be able to spot it in early spring when the leaves are tender and choice. The seeds can be gathered in late summer when they've dried on the stalk. The root can be dug anytime but is best harvested in fall after the plant has gone to seed. Because dock takes up a significant amount of minerals into its root, leaves, and stalk, be careful where you harvest and make sure the land is free of lead contamination or other heavy metals.

How to Gather

Harvest the tender leaves in spring and fall by hand or with kitchen shears. The leaves become tough and relatively uninteresting in flavor as the plant blooms and the weather becomes warm.

Dock blooms in late spring. Then in midsummer, the seeds ripen to a rusty brown. Dock's flower stalks are noticeably brown in the open fields among the evening primrose, blue chicory, and the tall but not yet flowering goldenrod. Gather the seeds on a dry day by the handful into paper sacks. In the kitchen, dry them completely in a dehydrator before storing. The root can be gathered and dug after the plant has gone to seed, then cleaned and stored for a few weeks in the refrigerator.

How to Eat

When small and tender in the spring, the greens are good eaten fresh, but for those who have yet to fully embrace and acclimate to the predominantly bitter flavor (yes, there are a few notes of citrus, but only in the early cool weather), try cooking the greens. This helps neutralize the bitter flavors and also releases minerals

Dock is plentiful throughout the Midwest, thriving in just about any open space with disturbed soil.

Dock seeds can be gathered when dry in summer for a nutritious addition to crackers and granola.

in the leaves. Stir-fries, frittatas, and egg dishes work well with dock. The greens can also be sautéed with garlic, onion, and other spring herbs like parsley, and then pureed and frozen into cubes for later use in soups—perfect for adding greens to the winter menu.

Brown dock seeds can be prepared as in recipes that call for buckwheat. The seeds can be ground and added as a protein to salads or soups, and even dehydrated and made into a nutritious cracker. For those interested in athletic performance, add the seeds to a wild granola of amaranth, chia, and wild nuts for extra plant protein.

Dock root is particularly high in iron and can be made into a molasses syrup that can serve as a substitute for the synthetic iron supplements available at the health food store.

Future Harvests

Dock reproduces easily with its prolific seeds. You can help it flourish by scattering the seeds along the way back to the kitchen for wildlife to gather.

elder

Sambucus nigra

berries, flowers

From lightly scented cordials and pound cakes made with elder flowers to yummy jam made from its dark and delicious berries, you will find harvesting, preparing, and enjoying the flowers and fruits of the elder to be a delightful high-summer experience.

How to Identify

Elder is a large shrub that begins bearing clusters of fruits when it is approximately 5 feet tall. Its bark is light gray with bumps, and its wood is brittle, unsuitable for building. Branches are hollow and filled with pith.

Elder's leaves are opposite and compound, with five to seven leaflets that are smooth, lance-shaped, toothed, and between 2 and 6 inches long. Around midsummer, the white fragrant flowers unfold in terminal clusters on showy umbels. The deep purple and black berries ripen in mid- to late August in a normal summer, hanging heavy from the umbels in the bush.

Where and When to Gather

Elder grows in hedgerows, along edges of fields, and in drainage ditches and other low-lying areas where water flows.

Gathering elder's flowers in a secret urban garden in the middle of July.

The umbel and leaflets of the elder.

Dried elderflowers make a wonderful tea and simple syrup perfect for flavoring sodas and desserts.

The first of the elder's flowers open after solstice, and blooms continue through mid-July. The berries appear in mid-August and are quickly eaten up by the birds.

How to Gather

Carefully gather the flowers by cutting umbels from the bush, taking care to gather only the open blossoms. Use large baskets or boxes to hold the umbels so they are not crushed, and lay them flat on a screen to dry. Separate the dry flowers from the stem and store for later use. Remember that the elderflowers you harvest now will mean fewer berries later. So balance out your harvest, particularly if elder isn't prolific in your area.

In mid- to late August, gather only the umbels that carry dark purple to black berries. The berry harvest has a tendency to bring along a host of spiders into the kitchen (although I find this less of a nuisance and more a part of its magic). The berries don't need to be washed; in fact washing can actually damage the very ripe, juicy berries. So take care to gather berries that are free of dust or bird droppings. It is important to separate the berries from the stems before freezing or drying as the stems have been known to cause stomach upset.

How to Eat

The elderflower and berry can be used both as food and valuable herbal medicine. When fresh, the elderflower has a fragrant, dusty odor. Honeybees adore the plant for its nectar and pollen, and in the kitchen, the flower pairs delightfully with honey. Consider infusing honey with elderflowers, or make a simple syrup for the bar using honey in lieu of cane sugar. The flavor of the elderflower is light and works well with other flavors that are equally light and not overpowering.

Notes of citrus work especially well with elderflower, particularly in drinks or in baked goods. The popular liqueur of St. Germain is made of elderflower, and a similar drink can be handmade using a neutral grain spirit with honey as a sweetener.

Jams, fruit leathers, and shrubs are all ways to use the small but sweet and tasty dark berry. The seed of the elderberry can be a nuisance, so remove it using a sieve for projects like jam or fruit leather. The berry can also be made into a simple syrup filled with antioxidants; use it in cocktails or as a base for the traditional vinegar and honey shrub or oxymel.

You can easily make a homemade elderberry syrup with neutral grain spirits and raw honey; fortify it with herbs like wild bee balm and yarrow. Not only is it more delicious than what you can find at the health food store, homemade elderberry syrup is much more affordable.

Either dry or fresh elderflower can make a delightful tea that performs as a relaxant, and it will incite a bit of sweating when enjoyed hot. Because of this, the elderflower is commonly used for colds and flu to support a productive fever and relax tension from body aches. It is such a sweetly mild tea that children easily take to sipping it, especially if they are under the weather. It mixes well with peppermint and even a bit of yarrow, in a classic gypsy tea recipe. Elderflower tea is also nice sipped in the evening, as a way to relax and prepare for bedtime.

Future Harvests
The fast-growing elder is prolific in hedgerows and ditches across the Midwest, and it is easily propagated by cuttings set out by the forager.

Elderberries are a classic herbal medicine used to fight off colds, flus, and other viruses, but they also make delicious jams, fruit leathers, and vinegar shrubs. The berries will be a dark blue-black when ripe and hang heavy from the umbels in the bush.

field garlic

Allium vineale

EDIBLE leaves, bulb

As the snow melts away in early spring, there's nothing more delightful than discovering wild herbs like field garlic. Its flavor is always a welcome addition to the table and a beacon that more fresh, wild flavors will be coming soon.

How to Identify

Wild field garlic is a cool-weather, clumping, perennial bulb. It's shade tolerant and grows in rich, well-drained soil along the edges of the fields and woods. A fail-safe identifier: the entire plant is edible and smells noticeably like a pungent, acrid, garlicky onion. The leaves are long and hollow, growing to heights of up to 36 inches.

The bulb of field garlic is small, growing usually not more than ¾ inch in diameter and 1 inch in length. When field garlic

Field garlic is one of the earliest spring herbs and can often be found when the snow melts back.

flowers in late spring, it produces a round head of small, purple, edible florets. It prefers cool weather and dies back in the spring but will return again in the fall with the rains.

Where and When to Gather
Look for field garlic in early spring emerging from beneath the leaf litter alongside trails and in the fields as the snow begins to melt.

How to Gather
Field garlic is a bulb, so remember that by harvesting the bulb, you are removing the entire plant from the soil. Clipping the edible tops is the more sustainable way to enjoy this plant. However, it is perfectly fine to wash, chop, and prepare both bulb and root for cooking.

How to Eat
Field garlic has a garlicky onion flavor. The green tops are delicious used in place of the grocery store variety of green onion in herbed salads and as a garnish. The bulb can also be used in cooking, but it can be fibrous if not pureed or cooked down to make it more tender. Both the bulb and tops add a welcome fresh and wild flavor in spring after a long winter of dry and grocery store herbs.

Future Harvests
While field garlic is more a weedy wild edible, be a mindful harvester if you wish to have access to field garlic each spring. Instead of harvesting the relatively small bulbs, choose to trim only the tops for kitchen projects. This will ensure a steady supply each year.

garlic mustard

Allaria petiolata

`EDIBLE` leaves

Abundant at the forest's edge, along roadsides, and on river floodplains, garlic mustard is deemed by many as a noxious, invasive species that chokes out native vegetation. But we mustn't forget that garlic mustard is also a highly nutritious spring green.

How to Identify

Garlic mustard is an early spring biennial. In its first year, it grows as a basal rosette of green, heart-shaped leaves. In its second year, the plant sends up as many as six flower stalks about 40 inches tall. The white flowers, each with four petals, grow in tight clusters. Seeds ripen and are dispersed in late spring and into early summer.

Where and When to Gather

Garlic mustard is shade tolerant and likes rich, well-drained soil. Widespread across the forest floor and along the edges of wooded areas, it is one of the first spring

Tiny basal leaves of a first-year garlic mustard plant. The entire plant will smell predominantly of garlic.

A tall stand of garlic mustard in bloom. The flowers produce thousands of tiny seeds, helping the plant spread easily in disturbed soil.

greens to be seen across the Midwest once the snow melts away. Both the first-year basal rosettes as well as the second-year plant are edible, until the plant begins to flower. As with many early spring greens, the flavors of garlic mustard are predominantly bitter. Different parts of the plant, as well the age of the plant, can affect the degree of bitterness. The early basal roots are more bitter in the spring, turning sweeter in the fall after a frost.

How to Gather

Frequently the entire plant is pulled before it goes to flower to help maintain control of the population. Try to work clean in removing the plant from the soil, as this will mean less soil to remove in the kitchen. If you don't remove the entire plant and only want to gather the leaves, kitchen shears can easily trim the edible greens. The stems are best harvested before the flower buds appear or open. Trim these succulent stalks of their leaves and discard the leaves before cooking.

How to Eat

The earliest appearance of garlic mustard was recorded in the mid-1800s on the Atlantic coast. High in vitamin C and a nutritious bitter green, it is believed to have been brought by settlers to the area of Long Island, N.Y., for food and medicinal purposes. Since that time, garlic mustard has spread south and west and has wreaked havoc on natural areas throughout the eastern United States, particularly in disturbed areas within fields, floodplains, and woodlands across the Midwest.

One of the most popular ways to prepare garlic mustard greens is as a versatile, delicious pesto. Pesto recipes can be adjusted (the lovely thing about pesto) to suit personal taste preferences and the flavor of the garlic mustard that is being harvested. Want to prepare a large batch? Pesto can be made without the nuts and frozen into ice-cube sized portions that will last for several months until the local basil is ready for harvest. Add the nuts later, when you are ready to serve the dish.

The pesto can be added to pasta, used in soups (like a French soupe au pistou), served on crackers with cheese as an elegant appetizer, or even used as a base for a wild foods pizza of local morels, homemade soft cheese, and wild onion. In other dishes, partner garlic mustard with complimentary flavors like parsley, walnuts, and lemon to suit your palate.

Future Harvests

Garlic mustard thrives on disturbed land and areas under development. It is a winter-hardy biennial plant and can reproduce lightning fast in its second year, able to produce hundreds of seeds once it goes to flower. Once the plant sets its seed, the seeds can remain viable in the soil for many years. So if you want to eliminate the plant, pull it before it sets out its showy white flowers. Be sure to replant the area with other plants native to the area to help reestablish the disturbed space and prevent another garlic mustard invasion.

ginkgo

Ginkgo biloba

`EDIBLE` leaves, nuts

Ginkgo is an ancient native tree, once distributed widely across both Asia and North America, and now commonly found as a landscape ornamental. The leaves make a healthy tea, and the nuts pair well with bitter foods and can be used in baking.

How to Identify

Ginkgoes in the wild are known to grow up to 100 feet tall, but it is more common to find the tree growing between 30 and 60 feet tall, particularly if it is planted as a landscape ornamental. Its bark is gray, and as it ages, it becomes cracked and deeply furrowed. The leaves are handsomely lobed and deeply veined, kelly green in summer and golden in the fall. There are male trees and female trees. It is most common to find the male trees planted as ornamentals, as the female trees produce a small, putrid-smelling, peach-colored fruit in the fall that makes a smelly mess along city streets and trails. The fruit, however,

Ginkgo leaves are uniquely shaped and textured, which makes them easy to identify.

Ginkgo leaves are ready to harvest for tea when golden yellow in fall.

contain a nutritious nut about ¾ inch across.

Where and When to Gather

While the ginkgo tree prefers rich, well-drained soil, it is drought tolerant and thrives in a variety of growing conditions, including polluted urban environments. The leaves of the ginkgo are ready for harvest when they turn a golden yellow hue in late fall, about the time of the first frost.

If you haven't identified the ginkgo by its unique leaf, then your nose might help you locate one in the late fall as the leaves change color. The putrid odor of the ginkgo fruit is unmistakable: it has a sharp, ripe smell, reminiscent of a rotting cheese (or a good smelly cheese, depending on your stance).

How to Gather

Gather from trees that are not in a main thoroughfare or in heavily trafficked urban areas. The leaves are easily collected by placing a sheet beneath a tree or branch and shaking the plant. Dry the leaves on a screen or in a food dehydrator for use in tea.

Wear gloves when you gather the female fruits as they fall to the ground (the compounds in the ripe fruit can irritate sensitive skin and cause a dermatitis-like rash in some people). Take the fruits back to the kitchen, and while still wearing gloves, remove and compost the pulp from the nut. Dry the green nut completely in a dehydrator or oven; then the edible green nut can be easily cracked open and shelled.

How to Eat

The ginkgo nut is promoted as a brain food, as it offers a mineral combination of phosphorus, potassium, copper, thiamine, and niacin. Once shelled, the nut should be roasted, toasted, or boiled to improve and maximize digestibility.

The ginkgo nut has a unique flavor with a lingering backnote of ripe cheese. It pairs well with bitter greens in salads, cheeses, and balsamic vinegars and dressings, as well as crisp white wine like a Pinot Gris.

The cooked nuts are a popular food in Asian dishes such as congee and egg custard. They are also a favorite of older Chinese women who gather in parks as the fruits fall from the tree.

While both the ginkgo nut and leaf are traditional herbal medicines in China and Asia, the leaf is popular in Western herbal medicine and is commonly found as a dry tea in health food stores, purporting benefits for brain health. The yellowed, dry leaves can be prepared for tea; boiling the leaves extracts the most minerals for the brew.

Future Harvests

Ginkgo is a common wild and ornamental tree across the Midwest, and you can gather the fruits and falling leaves without affecting future harvests.

Common city and landscape trees, ginkgoes are tolerant of excess city pollution. Gather the leaves and nuts in areas away from excess car and industrial pollution.

goldenrod
Solidago species

`EDIBLE` leaves, flowers

Goldenrod spreads across open fields in August as a stand
of brilliant yellow, providing a fruitful haven for honeybees.
Goldenrod's bright, astringent, and bitter flavor makes it a useful
herb for us, too, in brewing beer and flavoring beverages.

How to Identify

More than 20 species of goldenrod are
distributed across the Midwest, and all
possess similar properties and can be used
interchangeably. Goldenrod is a handsome
and stately native wildflower that blooms
in the sun of the high summer into early
fall. It is a clumping perennial that stands
up to 5 feet tall.

Goldenrod's oblong and lanceolate leaves
are arranged as basal rosettes. From the
rosette, oblong, silvery green, hairy leaves
alternate up the stalk. The plant blooms as
early as mid-August, and its small, hairy,
yellow flowers, arranged in dense sprays,
hang heavy in the summer sun.

Where and When to Gather

The Latin word for goldenrod is *solidago*,
with the root, *sol*, meaning sun. Honeybees will be busy in goldenrod beneath
the sunshine, gathering nectar and pollen,
and their activity signifies an opportune
time to gather the plant. Use your senses of
taste and smell to determine which plants
have the most aromatics.

How to Gather

Gather the full stalks of the leaves and
sprays of the flowers in warm, dry, and
sunny weather. Don't harvest the plant on
a wet and rainy day: it will be less aromatic
in damp weather. Drying the flowers can
be a challenge, as the aster-like flowers
will dry, go to seed nearly immediately, and
make a frustrating mess. Dry the hanging bundles within a loose-fitting paper
bag to catch the drying, opening, and puffy
flowers.

How to Eat

Goldenrod's flowers and leaves are aromatic and predominantly bitter. The plant
is also astringent, leaving your tongue
dry when you taste the leaves or drink
tea made from it. The flowers and leaves
can make a brightly flavored bitter useful in various cocktail recipes or summer
shandies. For beer brewers, goldenrod has
a pleasant combination of aromatic high
note (almost citrusy) and bitter that can be
a nice addition to a crisp Belgian-style ale
or other light-style brew. Add goldenrod in

Goldenrod's blooms offer delicious nectar to honeybees. It also gives us an aromatic and bitter spice that is useful for teas and beer-making.

the second fermentation of a brew process as the longer the process, the more prominent the bitter flavor becomes and the less aromatic it will be.

Future Harvests

Goldenrod is an abundant wildflower across the Midwest, and gathering a few bundles of flowers in the summer sun won't significantly harm the plant's future sustainability.

greenbrier

Smilax species

EDIBLE leaves, shoots, rhizome

Greenbrier is a sprawling vine, abundant across the Midwest and even deemed invasive by many naturalists. The tender shoots, tiny leaves, and new tendrils off the main stalks can be used as cooked spring greens, and its rhizome offers a starch that can be used for baking.

How to Identify

Many species of greenbrier grow across the Midwest. The perennial, evergreen shrub has tendrils at the axils of its shiny green, smooth, alternate, heart-shaped leaves. Blue-black berries form alternately in

Tender spring leaves and shoots of the sprawling greenbrier have a flavor similar to springtime asparagus when cooked.

clusters and ripen in late August. The rhizome of the greenbrier varies in size, but is white and knobby.

Where and When to Gather

Greenbrier is a shrub that can creep across vegetation and create dense thickets in wet, swampy land. These thickets provide wonderful habitats for wildlife. Gather the shoots and leaves in the spring and the rhizome anytime.

How to Gather

In the spring, use a knife or clippers of cut the new shoots and growth off the stalk. The tender spring leaves can also be gathered for cooking. The rhizome, which can be dug up anytime during the growing season, varies in size depending on species and soil conditions. To find the younger rhizomes, which are less fibrous, track the younger stalks of the vine back down to the earth and dig. Clean thoroughly in the kitchen and prepare fresh, or slice and dry in a dehydrator and store in an airtight container for later use.

How to Eat

The tender shoots, tiny leaves, and new tendrils of greenbrier can be sautéed and cooked in oil or butter, and seasoned like springtime asparagus. Greenbrier root should not be confused with the more aromatic root of the *Aralia nudicaulis*, or sarsaparilla, which is markedly more aromatic. The greenbrier's rhizome has a more starchy-sweet flavor that is slightly acrid.

The rhizome has a useful starch beneath its outside rind, which can be removed by a wet process (see cattail for further discussion of this process). The dried and preserved starch can be useful as a thickening agent in baking. The rhizome can also be cleaned and sliced thin for a batch of fermented pickles.

Future Harvests

Greenbrier is abundantly distributed across the Midwest and is considered invasive. Regular harvesting helps manage the plant's overgrowth in wetland areas.

groundcherry

Physalis virginiana, P. heterophylla

EDIBLE fruit

While it looks like a small yellow tomatillo, is a relative of the tomato, and has the word "cherry" in its name, the groundcherry is none of these things. It is a delicious fall season fruit that is very versatile in the kitchen for both sweet and savory dishes.

How to Identify

Groundcherry is a perennial plant in the nightshade family, growing to lengths of about 1 to 3 feet across the ground. It has alternate, green, hairy leaves and nodding, yellow, bell-shaped flowers. The deep yellow marble-shaped fruits are encased in five-sided husks formed by papery sepals similar to but smaller than the tomatillo. Groundcherries develop in late summer and ripen after a frost.

Where and When to Gather

Groundcherry thrives in full sun and tolerates many soil conditions. It is often found along the edges of sunny, open fields and urban lots in disturbed soil. Gather the fruits in the late fall, about the time of the frost, tasting the fruit to ensure a balance of tart and sweet.

How to Gather

Gathering a basket or two worth of groundcherries is usually easy to do in an hour's time. Remove the papery sepal in the kitchen and store the fruit in a dry vegetable bin in the refrigerator until use.

How to Eat

The groundcherry is a delightful fall fruit. Its savory and sweet flavors make it very versatile in many dishes, and it's marvelous in pies, jams, and chutneys. The groundcherry pairs well with herbal flavors of basil, thyme, or rosemary. Savory groundcherry jams and chutneys pair well with ripe and full-bodied local cheeses. The groundcherry can also be prepared as a savory salsa, and it stands up to the heat of a variety of chilies—perfect on grilled fish or tacos al pastor.

Future Harvests

Groundcherry is a plentiful perennial plant in open fields and waste places, and it reproduces easily from seeds of the fallen fruit. You can glean the groundcherry without significant worry of affecting future harvests.

Dry husks of the groundcherry in the fall contain ripe, yellow fruits inside.

ground ivy

Nepeta hederacea

creeping Charlie, gill-of-the-ground

EDIBLE leaves

Ground ivy is a common yard weed that is irritating to most people who want a perfect Kentucky bluegrass lawn. For the forager, however, ground ivy has a pleasant aroma and is useful as a spring culinary herb as well as an herbal remedy.

How to Identify

Ground ivy is a creeping mint-family plant, growing not much more than 6 inches off the ground. It spreads by runners and has square stems and small, soft, opposite, heart-shaped leaves. Small purple flowers bloom in late May, and the plant has a fragrant mint scent when crushed.

The leaves of ground ivy can be used as an aromatic tea or for a wild-flavored mojito.

Where and When to Gather

Ground ivy's minty aroma is noticeable in the spring when folks begin to cut their lawn. Interspersed with dandelions, dock, and grass, it sometimes grows thick like a carpet. Ground ivy is known to take up minerals into its stem and leaves, so gather in an area where you are familiar with the soil quality.

How to Gather

Ground ivy can easily be picked by hand or with kitchen shears, but take care to not also cut in grasses, or you will be picking out those blades in the kitchen. After ground ivy blooms, it will begin to die back a bit and turn dry and rough like many other mints. Harvest ground ivy as cleanly as possible, as it is difficult to remove embedded dust and debris from the small hairs on the plant, even with washing. Take note that washing will "wash" out the aromatics of the plant as well. Use ground ivy fresh as the aromatics are significantly lost upon drying or dehydrating. Other mints, like *Monarda* species, are better choices if you want to dry an aromatic mint-family plant for tea.

How to Eat

Ground ivy, with its minty flavor profile, can be added fresh as a culinary herb to many dishes, including spring herb salads, spring rolls, spring soups (like chilled locust blossom soup or a nice French soupe au pistou), or fresh spring pesto of arugula. The fresh plant can be muddled like garden mint into a mojito. As an herbal remedy, ground ivy is very helpful to alleviate head and chest congestion. Prepare the ground ivy as a hot tea (cover while steeping to preserve the aromatics). It also makes for a chest-clearing steam inhalation.

Future Harvests

Those who wish to have a perfectly groomed landscape often consider ground ivy a nuisance. Gathering it poses little threat to this dandy little "weed."

groundnut
Apios americana
wild bean, Indian potato, potato bean
EDIBLE tubers

Gather this nutty flavored, edible tuber for sautéing and roasting. The groundnut is high in plant protein and a delicious root vegetable to add to the forager's dinner table.

How to Identify

Groundnut is a sprawling vine that can climb up, over, and across considerable amounts of woodland vegetation. Its leaves are pinnate and compound, with five to nine smooth, ovate leaflets. The groundnut vine attaches to anything with its thin tendril stems, and it produces delicately beautiful two-toned, purple-mauve, fragrant flowers which are arranged in clusters that bloom in late July and into August.

The edible tubers are found immediately underneath the soil's surface and sometimes can be seen without digging in areas where there is running water. The tubers grow like potatoes do. They are connected by small rhizomes and can range from the size of a grape to as large as softballs. The outer skin of the tuber—the rind—is tan and surrounds a white, starchy inside. A white latex exudes from the cut tuber.

Where and When to Gather

Areas of groundnut can be spotted at a distance, and upon closer survey, you will notice that the ground is wet, as the groundnut loves the rich, well-drained soils of ditches and stream beds. Groundnuts can be found many places where you might see Joe Pye weed and elder. You will most likely see its tendrils and purple flowers wrapped around the branches of elder while you harvest elderberries. In some areas, spring streams will clean away open areas from which to harvest the tubers, making identification and harvesting easy.

How to Gather

The tuber can be gathered at any time of the year with a shovel. In an hour's time and in the right soil conditions, you can easily collect 30 to 40 pounds. The thickness of the tuber rind will indicate age, as the thicker the rind is, the older the tuber. The thicker rinds will need to be peeled in the kitchen before processing; the younger rinds can be left on. Wear kitchen gloves, as the milky latex can irritate sensitive skin. Store the cleaned tubers in a damp cloth or sack in the refrigerator or in cold storage.

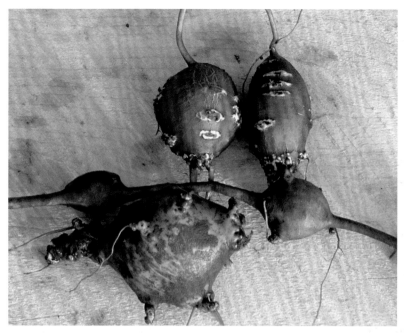
Groundnut harvests are abundant, and you can easily dig large basketfuls at one time.

How to Eat

The groundnut, as tubers go, has a nuttier flavor than a cultivated potato and is significantly more fibrous. This should be taken into account during its preparation. As a legume (in the family Fabaceae), the groundnut is high in plant proteins. As for grains and legumes, soaking the groundnut prior to cooking improves its digestibility, particularly for those are sensitive to legumes (those with noted allergies are advised to avoid the groundnut).

Chop or parboil the groundnut tubers before sautéing, roasting, or freezing to help break down the fibers of the food. It's a food that will add substance and protein density to any dish, of particular value if you want to decrease your reliance on animal proteins. The groundnut can be prepared in soups, stews, casseroles, and skillet meals with a variety of flavorings— Indian curry, Latin flavors, Asian soy and tamari, or French herbs. You can use it fresh or parboil and freeze it for use later.

Future Harvests

The groundnut actually thrives from additional harvesting. By mindfully tilling and turning the soil and breaking up the rhizomes, the forager allows the groundnut to propagate and spread. As a nitrogen fixer, the plant is an excellent permaculture crop. It is a good companion plant for berry crops that like moist but well-drained soil, and it restores soil fertility to the immediate area.

hawthorn

Crataegus species

maythorne, haw

EDIBLE fruits

Hawthorn's branches are spiked with long thorns, warning foragers to hone their senses and pay attention, lest they fall into the shrub's spiny clutches while gathering the delicious red fruits.

How to Identify

Hawthorn is a deciduous shrub that grows up to 30 feet tall, dependent on species and growing conditions. The bark is dark brown and scaly, with dense branches that have very long thorns, sometimes 3 inches or more long. The whitish five-petaled flowers bloom in mid-May, around Mother's Day. The red fruit, about 1 inch in diameter, hangs in clusters that ripen in early September.

Where and When to Gather

The hawthorn can be found in fields and in hedgerows. Once you begin to learn the tree's shape, you will be able to see it from afar, with its notable dense, seemingly wind-blown form. The red berries are ripe in early September.

How to Gather

Climbing a hawthorn to gather the berries is a silly plight. When the berries ripen, place a sheet underneath the tree and gently shake its branches to release ripe fruit from higher branches. Many *Crataegus*

species suffer from the rust blight that affects other Rosaceae family plants. This affects both the leaves and fruit, causing the leaves and berries to fall as early as August. The blighted fruit will still be edible but blemished and often not as juicy or ripe as the berries that are unaffected and remain on the tree until they are ripe.

How to Eat

High in flavonoids and antioxidants, the berries are an excellent food that can be used as you would crabapples in chutneys, jams, and pies. Be sure to process out the seeds. The hawthorn is also high in pectin and can be useful as a DIY pectin in canning recipes. Hawthorns, along with crabapples, can also be used in making a dry, hard cider.

Future Harvests

The hawthorn reproduces easily; birds are a big help as they love the fruit, too. Mindfully gathering the berry harvest will not significantly impact future harvests.

The fruit of the hawthorn can be used similarly to that of the crabapple in cooking and hard cider-making.

hazelnut

Corylus americana
filbert

nuts

Who can resist a dollop of homemade hazelnut spread atop a shortbread cookie made with a hazelnut extract and then dipped into a cup of steaming hot coffee flavored with a shot of hazelnut liqueur? Or perhaps a snack of curried hazelnuts and a hazelnut-wild onion hummus on a yellow dock cracker?

How to Identify

Hazelnut is a shrub that grows to about 20 feet tall. Its leaves are slightly hairy and alternate, with serrated heart-shaped sides. Both male and female flowers grow on the same shrub, producing catkins in the late fall and a scaly, greenish female flower in the spring. This ultimately

Hazelnuts ripening in the fall.

produces a smooth brown nut (or filbert) encased in the sticky green and pokey bracts of the flower and ripening in late fall.

Where and When to Gather
Look for the hazelnut in the shade in all manner of soil conditions. It grows at the edges of woodland and is often planted as an ornamental in parks and gardens. The nuts will begin to fall and be ready for harvesting in late September and into October.

How to Gather
Gather the nuts quickly in advance of the squirrels. Hazelnuts should be dried thoroughly in their brown hulls and then stored in a cool dry place until use. Remove the sticky bracts with gloves before shelling and use.

How to Eat
Hazelnuts are a delicious, versatile nut that can be incorporated into both sweet and savory dishes. As with chestnuts, dry roasting the hazelnut increases its toasted flavor and also helps with the nut's digestibility. Incorporate the hulled nut into salads; curry them for snacking; and puree them with wild onions, chickpeas, or maybe groundnut in lieu of tahini for a hummus-like sandwich spread.

One of the favorite and most known preparations of hazelnut remains the classic Nutella brand spread. This commercial product contains numerous fillers and stabilizers, so making your own spread out of foraged hazelnuts is genius. Take that one step further and transform your spread into a base for ice cream, or a hazelnut chocolate mousse.

Hazelnut baked goods are equally decadent. Chocolate brownies, chocolate flourless cake (be sure to add in some powdered foraged chaga and maybe some acorn flour as well), and tortes are just a few recipes that work well with hazelnuts. The French dessert dacquoise is a classic hazelnut recipe. Many recipes that call for almonds or pecans can also use hazelnuts as substitutes, as in the classic Linzer cookie or pecan sandy. Shortbreads shine with the addition of a homemade extract of hazelnut in lieu of almond extract. You can also produce a homemade hazelnut liqueur by easily extracting it (crush it, with the skin on) into brandy and sweetening it with maple syrup or honey.

Future Harvests
Help the propagation of the American hazelnut by planting saplings along the edges of mixed hardwood forests.

hibiscus

Hibiscus syriaca
rose mallow

EDIBLE flowers

The showy flowers of hibiscus or rose mallow are pleasing to the eye and refreshing on the palate as well. Hibiscus is brightly colored with a sour, tangy flavor, and it can be gathered for savory dishes and to make cocktails and drinks that are nutritious and high in vitamin C.

Hibiscus flowers can be gathered for flavorful simple syrups and tea.

How to Identify

Hibiscus is a perennial shrub that grows to 10 feet tall. Its dark green lobed leaves grow alternate along the branches. It's most known for its very showy, five-petal blooms, each from 2 to 4 inches in diameter, with colors that range from white to pink to purple.

Where and When to Gather

Because of its beautiful flowers, the hibiscus is frequently incorporated into landscape design. It is also frequently found on the sites of old homesteads and in parks, in partial to full sun in open spaces or along hedgerows. It blooms in mid- to late summer. Gather in areas free from chemical spray or lawn care treatment.

How to Gather

Gather the blooms of the hibiscus on a dry, sunny day. The flower wilts soon after picking. Dry or process it immediately.

How to Eat

Hibiscus is high in vitamin C and antioxidants. It can be dried for tea (warm or iced), and it blends well with black tea. Flavor hibiscus tea with cinnamon, spicebush berry, sarsaparilla, or sassafras for a more aromatic and spicy flavor. Hibiscus flowers make a delightful aqua fresca, and adding citric acid by means of lemon or lime changes the color of the tea to a brighter hue. If the flower used to make the tea has turned it pink, the addition of lemon will create a vibrant fuchsia.

A simple syrup made from the flower can be the base for many cocktails, from a spicy rum punch to margaritas and flavored champagne. The syrup can also be used in confections and baked goods as a flavoring and coloring agent.

The flowers can withstand cooking and are also delightful as a savory side dish. Lightly sauté the flowers with onion and garlic, and then incorporate them into an egg scramble or frittata. This mélange can also be used to top enchiladas to make a traditional Latin dish.

Future Harvests

A hardy perennial plant, hibiscus is considered invasive in some areas of the Midwest. The plant will easily propagate via cuttings. Gathering its flowers will not affect the plant's future harvests.

hickory

Carya ovata
shagbark hickory

EDIBLE nuts

The hickory nut is a common, native food that can be used in both sweet and savory dishes in your kitchen, from porridges and soups to cookies, cakes, and roasted foraged chai beverages. Add hickory nuts to your fall harvest calendar!

How to Identify

Hickory is a tall deciduous tree reaching heights of 50 to 70 feet. The distinctively shaggy bark (hickory is also referred to as shagbark hickory) consists of long, vertically oriented strips that break free of the trunk at one or both ends but remain attached in the middle. Strips may be 2 to 4 inches wide and up to several feet long.

Hickory leaves are alternate and

A bountiful hickory harvest.

Hickory nuts on the tree.

Bark of the hickory is "shaggy" and peels away from the tree.

pinnately compound with five to seven slightly hairy leaflets about 3 to 5 inches in length. Both male catkins and female flowers are present on the tree. The fruit, which ripens in late fall, is a light brown nut with a green, aromatic hull that is noticeably scored lengthwise and splits open as the nut ripens.

Where and When to Gather

Hickories are abundant across the Midwest. They naturalize in the woods along hiking trails, in the sides of the parks, and in many community settings. In the late fall, as the hickory's leaves turn a golden yellow, the nuts will begin to fall from the tree. Some will still be in their green hulls, while others will separate from their hulls and just show their brown shells.

How to Gather

Gather nuts that are without obvious insect damage, and return home for the more tedious task of shelling.

How to Eat

The hickory nut is a classic addition to cookies and hickory nut cake. It can be dehydrated and ground, then added to a nut flour-blend made with acorns, chestnuts, and amaranth seed. (Note that for a dough that rises and results in a fluffy baked product, you will need to add wheat gluten. Consult gluten-free baking resources for instructions on how to make a successfully rising flour.) With all this foraged goodness in the flour, go the extra measure to sweeten the dessert with maple syrup rather than cane sugar

Processing Hickories

The shelling of the hickory nut is an outdoor job. Wear proper eyewear protection. Carefully hit each nut (and not your thumb) with a hammer on the hickory's seam lines, which will cause it to fracture along the seam. Avoid smashing it into small pieces, sending fragments here there and everywhere and pulverizing the nutmeat in the process, increasing the likelihood that the hickory adventure will be abandoned altogether.

Carefully sort the nutmeat from the shell, then toast the meat. The nutmeats can be frozen for later use. No time to process the nutmeats in the fall? Freeze the nut whole and unshelled and process it later in the winter.

and use a local dairy or homemade hazelnut milk.

The hickory nut can be shelled, roasted, and boiled in milk or water to serve as the base for a hot chocolate or foraged chai with other foraged roots and spices. The green, unhulled nut is aromatic, like the black walnut and can be incorporated into a fermenting local nocino (see black walnut for details).

Future Harvests

Hickory is a native tree in mixed hardwood forests and is well distributed across the Midwest. Help maintain and protect the mixed hardwood ecosystem and prevent habitat loss to ensure the hickory's sustainability into the future.

honeysuckle

Lonicera japonica
Japanese honeysuckle

EDIBLE flowers

Honeysuckle grows wild over almost everything. Its succulent and sweet aroma resembles that of the intoxicating jasmine or orange blossom. The beguiling scent, captured as a culinary herb, makes a wonderful iced tea or decadently flavored infused honey.

The sweetly fragranced flowers of the honeysuckle smell like orange blossoms.

How to Identify

Several varieties of honeysuckle grow across the Midwest; here, we are speaking of *Lonicera japonica*, a vining plant with opposite, oblong, glossy leaves which can sometimes remain on the plant throughout winter, though it is not always evergreen in colder climates.

The flowers are white and tubular, and they form in pairs along the stem. The flower is very aromatic, similar in scent to jasmine or orange blossom, but its taste is predominantly bitter. The white flower fades to a light yellow as the flower ages. Its berries are black and inedible.

Where and When to Gather

Japanese honeysuckle is a rambling vine that loves to climb and appreciates hot, dry waste places. It blooms right at the solstice, apropos as it is a delightful plant to gather to help celebrate the sun's highest point of the year.

How to Gather

Pick the flowers by hand and as they quickly wilt, preserve them in honey or dry them for tea and store in an airtight container to preserve the sweet aromatics.

How to Eat

To preserve this seductive flower's enticing aroma, infuse raw honey with fresh blossoms. Simply gather fresh, unwilted blossoms and add them to a jar. Cover with raw honey and let infuse for at least several weeks, occasionally turning the jar upside down to stir up the plant material. The aroma seeps into the honey, which should be eaten in the most decadent manner, spooned over a good sharp cheddar cheese or perhaps a fresh goat cheese. It's also nice on toast. Serve the honey with or without the blossoms.

A cool infusion of honeysuckle—perhaps combined with rose petals, lemon balm, and garnished with fresh mint—makes for a refreshing and aromatic iced tea. A hot preparation of honeysuckle flowers (dry or fresh) reduces the aromatics slightly and makes for a bitter, relaxing tea.

Future Harvests

The vining honeysuckle is an invasive plant, and gathering the flowers will not affect its future growth significantly.

horsetail

Equisetum arvense, E. hyemale, and other species
mare's tail, snakegrass

EDIBLE stems

Horsetail is an ancient, mineral-rich plant. You can prepare it as a
nutritious broth that is neutral in flavor, so it can be incorporated
into a variety of dishes.

How to Identify

Horsetail is a perennial plant with tall
and erect stems that grow as tall as 3 to 4
feet. The stems are unique: jointed, dry to
the touch, coarse, and hollow. The stems
are either fertile or sterile. Fertile stems
appear in spring, are low growing, and
range in color from brown to white. The
sterile stems are green, grow taller, and
produce whorls of fine, feathery branches.
Both types of stem end in a dark head (or
strobil) at the top.

Horsetail grows in large stands along the banks of streams, rivers, and wetlands.

Young horsetail stalks in spring.

How to Use

Horsetail is high in minerals, specifically silica, which is foundational in maintaining healthy skin, hair, and nails. The flavor is neutral enough that it works in many combinations of other herbs. Horsetail can also be added directly to a simmering pot of bone broth and then strained off with the other ingredients before use.

Boiling fresh or dried horsetail to create a broth will extract the silica as well as the other minerals in the plant. This can be enjoyed as is or used in cooking to add minerals to other foods, especially starches and grains. Horsetail can be combined with other mineral-dense herbs like nettle, red clover, oat straw, and bull sea kelp. For those who have issues with bone density, arthritis, or connective tissue injuries, or for those who simply wish to rely less on synthetic sources of mineral supplements, horsetail is a plant to integrate into the kitchen.

Where and When to Gather

Horsetail grows along the banks of streams and rivers, in wetlands, and in dunes. The above-ground parts can be gathered anytime as needed, though traditionally the green sterile stems are gathered in the spring before the feathery branches unfurl in later summer.

How to Gather

Clip the upper parts of the stems with substantial kitchen shears or pruners, then cut the stems down to smaller sizes and dry them completely for storage in an airtight container. As with nearly all foraged plants, foraged horsetail is leaps and bounds better in quality than the dried horsetail available commercially.

Future Harvests

Clip the above-ground parts of the plant and leave its root system to ensure the plant's sustainability. Horsetail grows abundantly in wetland and dune areas, but habitat loss impacts its distribution.

Caution

Gather the plants in locales that are free from heavy metal pollution, as lead and other harmful minerals can be taken up into the stems of horsetail.

huckleberry

Vaccinium species

EDIBLE berries

Huckleberries are some of the most delicious berries to harvest in the summer. Head out for a hunt with basket and picnic in hand, and you will enjoy your summer foraging adventure. And your efforts may yield a huckleberry pie, milkshake, or even margarita.

Ripe huckleberries, irresistable.

How to Identify

Huckleberries grow in colonies, and species vary in height, ranging from a small 6- to 8-foot-tall groundcover in the woods to a towering, deciduous shrub of more than 10 feet in the open fields and bogs. All *Vaccinium* berries—including wild blueberries—are edible and interchangeable in use.

The bark of the huckleberry ranges in color and may have gray, green, or pink coloration on the woody stems. The leaves vary in size among the species, but most are 1 to 2 inches long, ovate, and simple, with smooth to slightly toothed edges. The whitish pink flowers bloom in late spring and give way to the delicious fruits that ripen in mid- to late summer.

The berry will be blue to nearly black and can range from ¼ to ¾ inch in diameter, borne singly or in small clusters. The berry's sweetness is both species- and season-dependent. The smaller berries have a tendency to be more sour than the large varieties, and weather has an effect on plumpness. Expect cooler weather to produce more sour berries, while warmer weather will encourage more sweet berries.

Where and When to Gather

The huckleberry harvest peaks in August. Seek them out in rocky outcrops, bogs, and sunny open fields. You'll also find them in the shade as groundcover in mixed hardwood forests and in the higher mountain elevations as you exit the Midwestern plains states. When you discover a stand of huckleberries, be ready for an abundance of picking.

How to Gather

Take a bucket and invariably some mosquito protection as you head out to gather these wild berries. Picking by hand is a slower approach than using a harvest rake but will guarantee a cleaner pick, with far fewer twigs, cast-off fruit, insects, and so on. Time saved in the field with the rake is then lost to sorting in the kitchen. Choose fruit that is free of bug damage, blight, or powdery mildew.

How to Eat

Turn the wild fruit into fruit leathers; make pies; dry the berries whole for winter snacking on porridge or oatmeal; make a crumble; or create a compote, jam, or cocktail syrup. One of my friend's favorite ways to enjoy the huckleberry is in a milkshake. I prefer a huckleberry margarita (pureed berries, good tequila, and on the rocks with salt). However you like them, no one can argue that huckleberry is anything but delicious.

Future Harvests

Most huckleberry stands offer an abundance of berries, but of course, always leave some fruit for wildlife. Be mindful not to trample lower ground that is covered by the plant. Habitat loss affects many areas where the huckleberry grows—particularly bog areas—so to help preserve these species, consider becoming active in ecosystem restoration and habitat preservation activities.

hyssop

Agastache scrophulariifolia

EDIBLE leaves, stems

With its showy purple flower spike of midsummer, wild hyssop is an aromatic herb that you can dry for a winter tea, or you can use its fresh leaves in salads, refreshing ice teas, flavorful simple syrups, and hard candies.

Hyssop in flower.

How to Identify

Hyssop is a clumping perennial mint-family plant. It can grow quite tall, up to 3 to 6 feet in height. It has square stems, opposite ovate and pointed leaves, and a long pinkish-purple flower spike that blooms in mid- to late summer. It is very aromatic and attracts many honeybees for its pollen and nectar.

Where and When to Gather

Wild hyssop loves damp soil and is found along the edges of woodlands in partly sunny areas, often alongside other native wildflowers like yarrow and wild bee balm. It blooms in mid- to late summer.

How to Gather

Take a stem here and there from each plant, taking care to not disturb the bees collecting nectar and pollen from the plant. The stems can be bundled and dried for tea. Store in an airtight container to preserve the aromatics.

How to Eat

The flavors of hyssop make for a delightful addition to a spring fruit salad. A cold infusion of hyssop with lemon balm, lavender, and rose petals are refreshing together as an iced tea. A hyssop simple syrup can be made for the cocktail cart and used in fun herbal martinis and summer drinks. Prepared as a hot tea, hyssop makes a lovely, soothing beverage that tastes delicious sweetened with honey. Add rose or elderflower to make an even more flavorful cup of tea.

Future Harvests

Wild hyssop isn't rare, but it also isn't as prolific across the Midwest as it once was. Habitat loss has affected this plant, and you can assist with its future sustainability by helping propagate the plant with cuttings. The honeybees will appreciate your effort.

Japanese knotweed

Polygonum cuspidatum

EDIBLE new shoots

Japanese knotweed is a non-native invasive plant that dominates many stream banks and ditches across the Midwest, making it a perfect foraging food. The early spring shoots are crunchy with a tart, citrusy flavor similar to that of spring rhubarb. Its bright flavors make for a tart simple syrup, good for use in cocktail recipes.

How to Identify

Perennial Japanese knotweed's woody, bamboo-like leafy stalks grow in dense stands, towering in heights up to 10 feet. The new shoots emerge in early spring and are hollow and jointed with red flecks at the joints along the stem. The leaves are heart-shaped, bright green, and arranged alternately along the stem. The plant goes to flower in late summer into early fall,

Young shoots of Japanese knotweed in spring, ready for cooking. Gather these smaller stalks until they are 8 to 10 inches tall; after that, they become woody and inedible.

Japanese knotweed is invasive and quickly develops large stands in areas of disturbed soil.

producing feathery clusters of dainty white blossoms.

Where and When to Gather

Japanese knotweed spreads voraciously, lining ditches, streambeds, and woodland fields where there is damp soil. To find a stand, look for tall stalks left from the previous year as their woody, jointed stems last well into the next season. Be sure the area where you harvest hasn't been treated with an herbicide meant to eradicate the plant. Look at surrounding vegetation for visible signs of plant burn, or ask the landowner or park manager about herbicide treatment.

How to Gather

The new shoots of Japanese knotweed emerge in early spring. Gather these smaller stalks until they are 8 to 10 inches tall; after that, they become woody and inedible. The stalks can be snapped off or trimmed with pruners.

How to Eat

The larger stalks can be peeled (unless you are cooking them, as the stalks soften significantly) and then prepared as you would use rhubarb in summer fruit compotes, jams, or pies. Because the fruit ripens much later than when you harvest Japanese knotweed, its stalks can be chopped and then frozen for later use.

Japanese knotweed is considered to be a natural laxative, so when you use it in recipes, take this into consideration (though the flavors of the stalks do tend to naturally limit its consumption).

Future Harvests

Japanese knotweed is at the top of nearly all invasive plant "Most Wanted" lists. It has virtually no known predator, other than foragers, to keep its spread in check.

jewelweed

Impatiens capensis

touch-me-not

`EDIBLE` stalks, flowers

Jewelweed is a citrus-flavored green with a bit of crunch. Its succulent and juicy stalks and flowers can be incorporated into soups and fresh spring rolls.

How to Identify

Jewelweed is a tall succulent annual plant that sometimes grows densely like ground cover. Its root system is shallow and its hollow stalk a neon translucent green, growing about 3 to 5 feet tall. The plant is very juicy when crushed. In July and August, jewelweed produces a beautiful tubular orange flower. It is a fast-growing plant that propagates by its abundant seed, easily released in the summer if anything brushes against the plant.

Where and When to Gather

Jewelweed is found along the edges of streams, ditches, and woodlands, and is

Jewelweed is a plant all foragers should know: it's a helpful herbal remedy that can be used to ameliorate contact with poison ivy.

Jewelweed spreads easily by seeds and grows quickly in large stands.

Poison Ivy: An Inevitable Foraging Companion

Poison ivy (*Toxicodendron radicans*) is a common invasive plant across the Midwest, found in damp riverbeds, woodlands, trailsides, sand dunes, and open fields. This is a tricky plant for foragers, who will get out into the field for early spring harvesting before the plant leafs out and unwittingly contract the rash. It's best to note where the plant grows before winter so as to avoid contact with the vines in the spring. "Leaves of three, let them be" may be a good start to identifying poison ivy, but the plant takes many shapes: a small creeping plant, with berries in the fall, or a bare hairy vine in winter. It has compound leaves, alternate along a woody stalk. It can be easily confused with box elder.

almost always in the same moist habitat alongside poison ivy. Drops of water that fall onto the leaves of the plant will glisten like jewels because of their waterproof, waxy coating which also gives a shimmer to the whole stand. For use in the kitchen for soups and stews, gather the plant before it flowers, from mid-June into July, when it ranges in height from 12 to 36 inches.

How to Gather

The plant has a shallow root system, so it's easily removed from the soil.

How to Eat

Jewelweed's stems are succulent and crunchy, with a density and texture similar to bean sprouts. To use in recipes that call for bean sprouts, use smaller jewelweed stalks or slice up the larger stalks lengthwise into more manageable sizes (large pieces can be fibrous). These pieces can make good additions to spring rolls or used to top spicy Asian soups. The leaves can be used in these dishes as well. If you want to use the greens in a cooked dish, add them at the end as they are tender and will cook down quickly.

Future Harvests

Jewelweed is prolific and is deemed by many as weedy. However, if you want to grow a jewelweed stand or spread the seeds, simply gather the ripe seed heads into a bag in the fall and sow the following year as an annual.

juniper
Juniperus species

EDIBLE berries, needles

The berry of common juniper is the predominant flavor note in gin. Both berries and needles can be gathered for use as a culinary spice in meat rubs and savory desserts, for spicing cocktails, and as a traditional herbal remedy.

How to Identify

Juniper is an evergreen shrub that grows up to 10 to 15 feet tall with dark red-brown shaggy bark. The leaves—or needles—are blue-green and highly aromatic. The fruits ripen in the fall into small, dusty blue, ¼ inch berries that dry to a dark black.

Juniper needles and berries—a chief flavoring agent in gin—can be used as a culinary spice and as a tea.

Juniper is a common wild shrub as well as a landscape planting.

Where and When to Gather

Juniper can be found in areas of rocky, dry soil in fields or as ornamental plantings. The aromatic berries will be ripe in late fall.

How to Gather

The leaves can be clipped with kitchen shears anytime, but are most aromatic in the spring. The berries, easily collected by hand, can be dried fully in a dehydrator, then stored in an airtight container to preserve the aromatics.

How to Eat

Juniper is a common curing spice in brines for red meat, fish, and pork. It's a common spice in curing gravlax, a Nordic raw salmon dish, and it makes a nice addition to a homemade mayonnaise or hollandaise sauce to top lamb, pork chops, tenderloins, or even vegetables. Juniper is a spice that works well in cabbage slaws, glazed Brussels sprouts, and glazed broccoli dishes.

Juniper can also flavor desserts; it works well with currants in a pâte de fruits or with cassis and dark chocolate in a mousse or pot de crème. As for the cocktail cart, juniper isn't just for gin. Juniper shines in a simple syrup for other cocktails. Consider making a juniper and garden sage simple syrup for citrusy summer cocktails, or an infused juniper maple syrup to use in rye whiskey drinks.

Future Harvests

Juniper is abundant across the Midwest but can be propagated by cuttings.

kousa dogwood

Cornus kousa

EDIBLE fruit

Kousa dogwood is a popular ornamental tree found in landscaping across the Midwest, and it has edible fruit that usually goes unnoticed. But for the forager, kousa's persimmon-like texture and taste makes it a delightful fall find.

Kousa fruit on the tree. Ripe fruit will be soft to the touch and detach easily from the branch.

Kousa is a common landscape plant whose fruit frequently goes unnoticed and unfortunately, ungathered.

How to Identify

Stunning as an ornamental dogwood, kousa is loaded with masses of showy white or pink blossoms in spring. These give way to a peculiar inch-diameter, ball-shaped fruit with the appearance of a giant raspberry. As the fruits ripen in the fall, leaf color deepens to a flame red.

Kousa is related to the common dogwood and has a similar graceful shape, growing up to 20 feet tall. Its bark is smooth and gray, and its leaves smooth, ovate, opposite, and parallel veined. The flowers are also similar to those of common dogwood, four-petaled and white, with some cultivars producing pink blossoms. The unusual fruits ripen in September and October to a textured reddish pink on the outside with an orange fleshy interior and a small seed.

Where and When to Gather

As an ornamental tree, kousa will be found in gardens, parks, and courtyards. Of course, always ask for the permission of the landowner before gathering if the tree you spot is in a private space. The kousa fruit is ripe when soft to the touch in September and will begin falling to the ground then. The inside of the ripe fruit will be dark orange, slightly astringent, and taste similar to persimmon.

How to Gather

Gather the fruits by hand, avoiding any with broken skin and taking care not to crush them while gathering. Unless the fruits have fallen in the dirt, it is not necessary to wash them. The fruits can be stored in the refrigerator for a few days before processing; otherwise dry, freeze, or cook them.

How to Eat

Kousa fruit can be prepared like you would a persimmon. Process through a food mill to remove the seeds, and then puree it into a thick sauce that can be used for fruit leather or baked into breads. The flavors work well with dark sweeteners like molasses, maple syrup, and brown sugar. It also pairs well with red fruit flavors like cherry, pomegranate, and cranberry. The fruit can be rough chopped (remove the seeds) and stirred into a chutney or made into a sauce to put atop pork, duck, prosciutto, and strongly flavored cow and goat cheeses. Curry spices also work well with kousa.

Future Harvests

Kousa is a common landscape tree, and gathering its fruit in the fall will do little to affect future harvests. It tolerates the growing conditions of the Midwest and can be easily propagated into permaculture landscape plans or anyplace tolerated by the flowering dogwood.

kudzu
Pueraria montana

EDIBLE shoots, leaves, tendrils, flowers, tubers

Kudzu is a nonnative, vining, and invasive plant that is known as the "plant that is eating the South." But you can eat it, as the shoots, leaves, tendrils, flowers, and tubers are all delicious, which helps reduce the abundance of the plant, even if only a little bit.

How to Identify

Kudzu is an Asian native plant that rapidly covers nearly anything, including all surrounding vegetation, with its creeping vines. The trunks of the vines are woody and normally range in diameter from 2 to 4 inches, but they can grow as wide as a foot. The leaves are trifoliate with ovate leaflets.

Kudzu's young leaflets can be prepared as greens in a variety of dishes including frittatas, quiches, and stir-fries.

The plant attaches itself to surrounding structures and vegetation with its stems and tendrils.

The pink and mauve flowers bloom in clusters in late spring, then bear long, hairy, and inedible pods in late summer. The vines are elongated and can grow to 5 to 7 feet in length (especially in the South).

Where and When to Gather

Kudzu is so abundant in the warmer southern zones of the Midwest that finding a substantial stand in that region is not a problem. Gather tender shoots, young leaves, flowers, and tubers away from pollution and soil contamination. If gathering from a park or property with a landscape management company, check to see if the stand has recently been treated with an herbicide (evidence of plant burn on surrounding vegetation will usually but not always help you identify this as well).

How to Gather

Look for new shoots and greens in early spring. Collect plenty, as you can process them for later use. Kudzu blossoms in early June, when you can gather entire flower clusters. The tubers can be gathered any time, particularly if the plant is being dug and removed completely from the soil to eradicate it from the area. Choose the smaller, younger tubers as they will be less fibrous.

How to Eat

Kudzu is as versatile to eat as it is invasive. Eat the tender young sprouts and spring greens in a variety of dishes including frittatas, quiches, and stir-fries. As they have a nice snow pea flavor, the greens work well in spring soups and blanched for spring rolls and chilled rice noodle dishes. The blanched leaves and shoots can be frozen for later use, so harvest them in abundance when they are unfurling and preserve the bounty for later.

The flowers, with their grape bubble-gum aroma, are equally versatile in the kitchen. They can be candied like violets for confections, made into an aromatic simple syrup for vodka cocktails (add a bit of lavender to the herbal syrup to balance its sweet fragrance), or turned into an aromatic jelly. The flower clusters can be made into fritters topped with goat cheese.

The tubers are a good source of starch. To prepare, use a dry process method (similar to how cattail starch is prepared). Use the starch for thickening stews or for baking.

Future Harvests

Kudzu is an extremely invasive plant and would remain bountiful even if it was gathered and processed commercially. If you gather it, you're helping with eradication.

lamb's quarters

Chenopodium album
wild spinach
EDIBLE leaves, seeds

Lamb's quarters has a mild, neutral flavor for greens. Because of their nutritious mineral content, stirring these wild greens into a meal is a great way to add nutrition to any dish.

How to Identify

Lamb's quarters is a common annual plant found in disturbed soil, fields, and waste places. It grows as tall as 5 feet high, with silvery, alternate, diamond-shaped leaves. Smaller, elliptically shaped leaves grow immediately beneath the primary leaves. Lamb's quarters blooms in midsummer

Lamb's quarters, or wild spinach, is a delicious cooked green.

Lamb's quarters is common in urban lots. The plant may take up heavy metals and nitrates, so be sure to harvest from a pollution-free area.

with small green blossoms arranged in branching clusters. The edible seeds are small, shiny, black, and ready to harvest by mid-September. The plant is not aromatic and has a neutral green flavor similar to spinach.

Where and When to Gather

Lamb's quarters is drought tolerant and can grow abundantly in poor quality soils. The plant can be gathered across the season.

How to Gather

Early in its growth, the entire plant is still tender and both leaves and stems can be gathered. As the plant grows across the season, the stem becomes woody. But the leaves can still be used—just trim the leaves off the stalk by hand then. The seeds can be gathered, but it is a tedious process. You'll probably choose to focus on

other seeds which are more abundant and will give you a greater return on effort, like dock seeds.

How to Eat

Lamb's quarters is best prepared as a cooked green. Sautéed in butter, lamb's quarters greens work well atop a pizza, integrated into a vegetable lasagna, or stirred into scrambled eggs or quiche. Add them to a risotto or wrap them into enchiladas. The greens work nicely in spring soups, especially with new potatoes as in a traditional Irish colcannon soup or creamy leek soup. Blanch and freeze the greens to preserve them for later use.

Future Harvests

Lamb's quarters grows abundantly in waste places. You can easily propagate it by scattering seeds in the fall.

lemon balm

Melissa officinalis

EDIBLE leaves, flowers

With its lemon-fresh scent, lemon balm is a delicious common culinary herb useful in cooking, baking, and herbal beverages.

How to Identify

Lemon balm is an herbaceous, perennial mint-family plant, growing to heights of up to 3 to 5 feet. Lemon balm is easily identifiable with its bright green, opposite, and fuzzy heart-shaped leaves arranged along a square stem. Lemon balm flowers in midsummer, producing whorled, white flower clusters that then bear small nutlets in late summer. The scent of the plant is unmistakable. It smells similar to lemon-scented furniture polish because of its citronella-like chemical compounds.

Where and When to Gather

Lemon balm loves the dappled sun at the edges of the woods. The tender leaves of spring are best to gather fresh for tea, as

Lemon balm leaves and flowers can be used for a relaxing herbal tea.

they are filled with a lemony citronella aromatic then, though the plant can be gathered as needed across the season.

How to Gather

Gather lemon balm in large bundles and then dry for tea, or use in the kitchen fresh for a variety of preparations. The plant goes to flower in midsummer and then to seed in August, resulting in a significantly drier plant to the touch. In the fall, new leaves appear that are as tender as the spring's leaves, but not nearly in the same quantity.

How to Eat

Traditionally lemon balm is used as a calmative tea. A hot tea of lemon balm is significantly more relaxing and more bitter than a cool infusion of the fresh plant straight out of the garden. Adding lavender, catnip, rose petals, and chamomile to the cool infusion of lemon balm makes a wonderful iced tea that also works well with a splash of vodka and fresh lemon wedge.

Use lemon balm fresh in brines and garnishes for light fishes, pork, and chicken. It pairs well on meats with other spring herbs such as fresh chives, chervil, parsley, juniper, and lovage, and it makes the most delightful addition to spring herbed butters.

In baking, lemon balm can be incorporated with herbs like lavender into light, buttery scones, and it also can be turned into an aromatic jelly.

For the bar, lemon balm simple syrup is great in refreshing spritzers or served as the base for a honeyed vodka cocktail. Steep fresh lemon balm into (cheap) white wine to give it a crisp, lemony flavor similar to that of a nice Viognier or Pinot Gris.

Future Harvest

Lemon balm is a voracious spreader, but not with runners like many assume. Lemon balm's nutlets spread easily, and you can help propagate the spread of the plant by gathering and planting the seeds in fall or starting them indoors. The plant can also be propagated by cuttings.

lilac

Syringa vulgaris

EDIBLE flowers

Lilac is one of those magical scents of spring. But don't relegate it to only cut flowers. Gather its blossoms and bring them into the kitchen, preserving their fragrance for use in drinks, confections, and desserts.

How to Identify

Lilac is a European shrub that grows to heights of 15 feet. It has dense branches with bark that is smooth and gray when young. As the branches grow older and larger in diameter, the bark becomes grayish brown and shreds. The leaves are simple, ovate, green, and shiny. Lilac blooms around Mother's Day, with showy flower heads (panicles) of sweetly aromatic and edible flowers that range in color from white to purple.

The fragrant blooms of lilac make delicious jellies and simple syrups.

Lilac bushes are easy to identify in late spring, with showy flower clusters that range in color from white to deep purple.

Where and When to Gather

Lilac is commonly planted as an ornamental, but it can also be found growing wild along hedgerows and fences.

How to Gather

Collect the flower heads (be sure to ask if you are gathering from someone's private garden) on a dry sunny day. In the kitchen, process them immediately, as the flowers quickly wilt and do not tolerate refrigerated storage for a significant amount of time.

How to Eat

Lilac has a memorable springtime scent that can be captured in an aromatic simple syrup or lilac jelly. Lilac syrup can be used in refreshing cocktail recipes, lemonades, and soda spritzers.

Lilac jelly can be used on pastries, shortbreads, or as an accompaniment (with fresh flowers as a garnish, of course) to French madeleines. It can also be drizzled over fresh spring goat cheese with spring chives for a savory and beautiful appetizer.

The flower's scent can be infused directly into white sugar (let infuse for two weeks to allow the aromatics to scent the sugar) and then used for baking projects. It's particularly delightful in shortbreads and sugar cookie recipes, and it would be delicious as a light flavoring in ice cream or plain yogurt.

Future Harvests

Lilac is a common plant across the Midwest, but you can propagate it with cuttings or from seed.

mallow

Malva neglecta

EDIBLE root, leaves, stems, flowers, seed-wheel fruits

Mallow is a nutritious spring vegetable, high in mineral content and versatile as a wild green. Like okra, mallow is especially useful in thickening soups and stews, like a foraged filé powder.

Mallow is a healthful cooking green as well as an herbal remedy.

How to Identify

Mallow begins life as a basal rosette that emanates from a taproot. Its rounded kidney-shaped leaves have scalloped edges, long stems, and a velvety feel. They are arranged alternately along a fleshy, slight hairy stem. The flowers are white with five petals, and the petals may be faintly streaked with pink or purple lines. Its root is spindly and white.

Where and When to Gather

Mallow is a persistent plant, drought tolerant, and often found in waste places with soil that is rocky and dry. Mallow's stalk and leaves are high in minerals so do not gather from potentially contaminated areas.

How to Gather

The root, leaves, stems, flowers, and seed-wheel fruits of the common mallow are edible all season; however; they are most tender and delicious in early spring. Gather the green tops with scissors and dig the root with a small hand tool. The plant can be used fresh or dried in a dehydrator for later use (even reconstituted, the plant still retains a high amount of mucilage).

How to Eat

Mallow is packed with minerals, which makes the leaves a good green to include in spring cooking, in dishes such as frittatas or stir-fries. Mallow has a unique texture that is similar to that of okra or sassafras. Add leaves to gumbo as a foraged filé powder or to Moroccan stews as a thickener. Mallow leaves and/or root can make a goopy tea using cool water. This tea can calm and soothe a scratchy, hot, dry throat and can relieve a dry cough.

Future Harvests

Mallow is well distributed across the Midwest and is characterized as a weed. It is easily propagated by cuttings and seeds if you wish to do so.

milkweed

Asclepius syriaca

EDIBLE shoots, flowers, flower buds

Milkweed is not only a favorite of the monarch butterfly but of the forager as well, as it offers tender shoots, edible flowers, and succulent flower pods for gathering through the spring and summer seasons.

How to Identify

Milkweed is a native perennial plant, emerging from the soil in spring with tender shoots. The hollow stems and green, ovate leaves have a slightly hairy texture. The leaves have green veins on both sides and are larger toward the bottom of the plant. Flower buds begin to form in early spring and are arranged in a rounded umbel shape, each unripe bud about ¼ inch in diameter.

The fragrant and showy flowers begin to open in late June to early July and are beautiful individual crowns of pink and white. Pods develop soon thereafter, hanging down from the stalk on short stems. These

The milkweed flower makes a fragrant simple syrup.

The unopened flower buds of milkweed can be pickled and have a texture similar to capers.

grow to be 3 to 5 inches long, are firm to the touch, and contain seeds and silks that ripen into late fall. The plant's seed pods and skeleton weather winter and can be found intact well into the spring. The entire plant exudes a milky white sap when cut or crushed that, while not poisonous, can cause dermatitis on sensitive skin.

Where and When to Gather

Milkweed grows in abundance across sunny fields, prairies, hedgerows, and farmsteads. The resilient stalks of the plant tolerate most winters, so that last season's stalks make a hunt for the spring-time shoots easy. The shoots are ready in early spring, the flowers can be picked in early summer, and pods are ready midsummer.

How to Gather

The new shoots push up through the soil in late April into early May, about the same time as wild asparagus. And like asparagus, the small shoots of the plant can be cut, gathered, and processed in the kitchen before they grow too large; after they are 8 to 10 inches tall, they become too fibrous.

The small, tightly formed circular buds of milkweed flowers begin to form in mid-June, and as they open they have a distinct appearance of broccoli florets, without the brassica flavor. Be sure to shake out any small insects, as they love to burrow in between the crevices of the buds. The unopened buds can be pickled like capers.

The flowers open in July and attract all sorts of pollinators. Milkweed is especially

Milkweed pods, ready for harvest.

neutral flavor. Why most wild-edible literature refers to milkweed as bitter is unknown to me, as they are unlike other truly bitter greens like chicory, wild lettuce, or dandelion. Because of their neutral flavor, the shoots are versatile with herbs and in spring soups, quiches, egg casseroles, and other dishes.

An abundance of greens can be parboiled and frozen for later use. The buds can be tossed into stir-fries or soups, and even pickled like capers. The fragrant milkweed flowers can be turned into a cocktail syrup to flavor a crisp summer white wine, soda spritzer, or lemonade. The flowers can also make a jelly suitable for toast, cheeses, and light fish. The pods make for excellent frying, dredged in flour, and cooked in oil, but they can also be parboiled and added to soups or stir-fries with their light green and pleasant flavor.

A cautionary note: excessive snacking on raw plant parts of *Asclepius syriaca* may cause indigestion in some people.

Future Harvests

Milkweed is a perennial plant and is abundant across the Midwest; however, increasing habitat loss is a concern. Depending on the size of the stand, small harvests of the shoots, flowers, or buds won't significantly affect future growth of the plant. Take care to select only a small portion of an established stand, and be sure to leave enough pods to help grow the stands for future harvests.

known for its ability to attract the monarch butterfly. Gather the flowers, shake out insects, and process fresh in the kitchen.

Milkweed pods begin to grow and ripen as early as late July. For eating, choose only small, immature pods with interior silks that are underdeveloped and white. Larger pods (above 2 inches or so) can be used, but the seeds and silks should be removed before cooking, and even then they can be too fibrous for most. Harvest and use fresh immediately, or parboil and freeze for later as the pods have a short shelf life.

How to Eat

Boil tender milkweed shoots and new leaves in water, and then use them as you would asparagus. The shoots have a more

monarda

Monarda fistulosa

EDIBLE flowers, leaves, stems

Not only should corn be knee high by the 4th of July, but the fiery pink blossoms of monarda open up right in the height of the summer sun. It is a spicy and aromatic herb similar to oregano and can be used similarly in cooking.

How to Identify

Monarda fistulosa is a perennial native plant, from the mint family. Typically 24 to 36 inches tall, it grows in patches in sunny open fields and prairies, often interspersed with black-eyed Susan, Queen Anne's lace, and goldenrod. *Monarda fistulosa* is a relative of common bee balm (*Monarda didyma*) and also of spotted bee balm (*Monarda punctata*) and can be used interchangeably in both cooking and herbal medicine. The stem is square, and the leaves are opposite and slightly toothed and hairy. The blooms of monarda are showy, with individual pink blossoms radiating from the center seed head.

Monarda blooms in full sun right around the 4th of July.

Monarda grows in perennial stands. Its leaves can be used as a culinary seasoning similar to oregano.

Where and When to Gather

The fresh spring leaves and stems of monarda can be gathered anytime and used in the kitchen fresh or dried. The summer's blossoms can be gathered and used until they become dry in the fall.

How to Gather

In summer, the stems can be gathered, bundled, and dried for use as tea in the winter. Store all fully dry plant material in airtight containers to preserve the aromatics.

How to Eat

As a culinary spice, monarda can be included in recipes calling for Italian seasoning combinations, such as pizzas, pasta sauces, and chili. Infusing this spicy herb into olive oil can result in a versatile aromatic oil that can be used as a dipping oil for breads and as a base for salad dressings.

Monarda can be infused into cold water for a refreshing summer iced tea. When it's prepared as a warming tea, the spicy aromatics can dispel the damp chill of a

Dried monarda blossoms make a delicious aromatic tea.

rainy day and can stimulate circulation in cold hands and feet.

Monarda leaves and flowers can be extracted in raw, local honey and served on toast or as a complement to a platter of fresh, local goat cheeses and bries. The honey can flavor meringues, cake icings, tea cakes, and other baked goods.

Future Harvests

This easy-to-grow perennial is a pollinator magnet, so it's important to preserve it. Depending on the size of the stand, do not cut down full plants for their stems, as nothing will be left for butterflies and honeybees. Monarda can be propagated by cuttings as well as by transplanting clumps in the fall. Preserving open space for native wildflowers will also support the long-term survival of this beautiful plant.

motherwort

Leonurus cardiaca

EDIBLE leaves, flowers

Motherwort grows abundantly in garden beds, along trails, and in open fields. It can lend its bitter flavor to cocktails, and it mixes well with aromatic plants like lavender, chamomile, and lemon balm for herbal cocktails and relaxing teas.

How to Identify

Motherwort is a biennial plant. The first-year leaves grow in a basal rosette. The leaves are deep green and mostly palmate and deeply lobed, with some variations. It is a mint family plant, and the stem is square. Its leaves grow in a whorled, opposite pattern up the stem. The blossoms, which appear in July and are favorites of honeybees, are showy pink clusters along the stem.

Early spring leaves of motherwort's basal rosette.

The flowers, opposite leaves, and square stem of motherwort make it easy to identify.

How to Gather

Gather motherwort leaves on a dry day, selecting plant material free of dust and debris. The leaves can be dried on screens for later use or prepared as a plant extract.

How to Eat

The flavor of motherwort is markedly bitter—it is not aromatic—so it can be extracted into vodka or Bénédictine liqueur to make a nice bitters blend. A motherwort-infused B&B (Bénédictine and brandy) can be sweetened with honey to make a nice elixir that can be added to tea or blended into herbal cocktails—think lavender martini with a dash of motherwort B&B bitters. Motherwort can also be used as a relaxant tea mixed with other herbs, especially aromatics like chamomile, lavender, and lemon balm to round out the flavor.

Where and When to Gather

Motherwort tolerates many soil conditions and can be easily found in open fields, along trails, in disturbed areas, and in garden beds (where it is usually identified as a weed). Gather the new leaves of motherwort in early spring; they will be strongly bitter, with little aromatics. The flowers can be gathered as well during their bloom time in July.

Future Harvests

Motherwort is a hardy biennial plant that grows nearly everywhere. It propagates prolifically from seed and can be transplanted easily. Gathering basal leaves and flower spikes won't significantly impact future harvests.

mulberry

Morus alba, M. rubra

`EDIBLE` berries

Compared to other summer fruits, mulberry has a slightly unremarkable flavor—it isn't very sweet or tart, and it isn't significantly jammy. That said, perhaps the delight of encountering such an abundant berry— especially in urban areas—makes it a special summer treat. It is a nice, cooling berry to snack on while you're out on the trail or on a run.

How to Identify

Mulberry is often most noticed as a small tree about 25 to 30 feet tall (though it can grow as tall as 70 feet). Its young bark ranges from yellowish brown to orangish brown, with scattered large white lenticels. Older bark is brown and ridged with an occasional glimpse of orange inner bark. If

Mulberry fruit ripening on the tree.

Mulberry trees are common along trails and grow wild in cities and parks.

the roots are unearthed by erosion or contraction, you will see that they are distinctively orange.

The leaves of both species are alternate, simple, more or less heart-shaped, and palmately veined with three main veins; they have rounded teeth along the edges. Both white and red mulberry trees may have mitten-shaped leaves. Leaves of white mulberry (*Morus alba*) are dark and shiny on top and feel smooth. Those of red mulberry (*M. rubra*) are not shiny and feel rough. Its fruits are longer, juicier, and better tasting than the white.

Where and When to Gather

White mulberry is a common ornamental planting in gardens, courtyards, and municipal parks across the Midwest, and it has naturalized in some areas. Red mulberry is commonly found at the edge of the woods and along trails, in partial sun and shade. Around the summer solstice, the juicy fruits of the mulberry can cause a mess wherever they fall, staining everything they touch with their black juice.

How to Gather

Mulberry fruit is easy to gather. Pick the berries by hand and place them into a bowl as the fruit is delicate and will not withstand being thrown into a bag or harvest basket. Note that the fruit will stain your hands, the container bowl, your clothing, and your shoes. (A quick wash with white vinegar removes most berry stains.) The berries do not have a long shelf life and should be eaten fresh or processed for later use in the kitchen right away. Remove the stems and freeze the clean fruit.

How to Eat

Mulberries are one of the first berries of summer to harvest, as well as one of the easiest to discover and gather for simple snacking or cooking, especially for the urban forager. The fruit is high in antioxidants and can be gathered in large quantities. Strain the berries through a sieve to make juice that then can be used to make a cocktail syrup. Flavor the syrup with herbs like lemon balm, basil, or even lemon verbena.

The mulberry harvest can be made into jam and fruit leather (run it through a food mill to remove the more seedy bits and fruit stemlets). Mulberries can also be baked into a pie alone or mixed together with the first of the summer strawberries. If used alone, the fruit can be quite runny, so add in an appropriate thickener to make sure the pie is not too soupy.

Future Harvests

Mulberry is an abundant and common plant. There's no need to worry about future harvests, as the seeds are spread by birds who also love the fruit. Mulberry also makes for an excellent edible landscape tree and fits well into a permaculture landscape design.

nettle

Urtica dioica
stinging nettle
`EDIBLE` leaves, stems

If you like spinach, you'll love nettles. Nettles have a flavor similar to that of spinach and are a versatile green to add to pizzas, pastas, frittatas, or egg scrambles. They are even more nutrient dense than spinach and are high in minerals and plant protein.

Nettle among the flowerbeds in downtown Detroit.

How to Identify

Nettle is a perennial, deep green plant that reaches heights of 7 feet in rich, nutrient-dense soil. Its opposite leaves are oblong, dark green on top and lighter green underneath, covered in fuzzy hairs, and roughly toothed and deeply veined.

One of nettle's chief identifiers is its sting. Stinging nettle doesn't really have stingers or thorns, but instead has fine, hollow hairs filled with formic acid that break open on the skin. The stinging, pins-and-needles sensation and hive-like bumps that can occur from handling nettle are caused by these hair-like needles found along the stem and leaves. The sensation is similar to the feeling you might get if fiberglass was rubbed on your skin. The hairs occur up and down the stems and on the undersides of the leaves. The severity and length of the irritation depends on the individual. Excess exposure to the formic acid can cause redness and welts on the skin that can last up to 36 hours. The juice of the plant can neutralize its sting; crushed dock leaves or jewelweed stalks can take the sting away. Drying or cooking the plant will cause the formic acid to dissipate.

Where and When to Gather

To find nettle, go on springtime (April to June) or late fall (October or November) hunts in areas of nitrogen-rich, damp, and well-drained soil. Pick the tender leaves and stems in early spring and late fall, both before and after the plant goes to seed.

As it likes damp soil, nettle can often be found adjacent to rivers, streams and lakes, springs, ditches, and wetlands, and along drainage areas. Know the area from which you are harvesting and its history of use—avoid areas adjacent to or downstream from large factories and farms.

How to Gather

Wear harvesting gloves and long pants to minimize the potential for skin irritation from the nettle's sting. Use gloves when harvesting in the field and processing in the kitchen. As the stems can get very tough and woody as the plant ages, choose to harvest plants with smaller, more tender stems, or harvest earlier in the spring season when nettle is most delicious. The upper stalks can be collected at about 18 inches in length; this is a great size to bundle and dry. Otherwise, the leaves and stems can be chopped for drying, freezing or used fresh in cooked dishes. The nettle sting will dissipate upon cooking.

To dry, spread chopped or whole nettle onto racks (window screens are great for this task), and let everything dry completely before storing the nettle in glass jars. If they are not completely dry before storage, they can mold. The full nettle stalks can also be bundled and hung to dry in a protected spot and then stored for later use.

By midsummer, nettle goes to seed and can reach a height of at least 5 to 8 feet. Nettle can still be foraged at this time for greens, but select plants that haven't gone to seed or flower.

Nettle's sting comes from small hairs on the leaf and stem, which cause a histamine reaction in most people. This effect is neutralized when the plant is cooked or dried.

How to Eat

Nettle can be eaten fresh in cooked dishes or dried. Fresh nettles can easily replace spinach in recipes that call for greens. It can be lightly sautéed and added to soups, egg scrambles, quiches, or other similar recipes. Nettle-friendly dishes include spanikopita, lasagna, risotto, stir-fry, pesto, and a creamy nettle soup.

The dried leaves can be enjoyed year round, added to soups and brewed as a mineral dense, tea-like beverage. To best extract the minerals of nettle, the leaves can be boiled to speed the mineral extraction time, or they can be left to steep overnight. Add a bit of honey to sweeten to taste, and you've created a refreshing, nourishing beverage that can be consumed daily. Nettle-infused vinegar extracts the minerals from the plant, and this is a great addition to the pantry for salad dressings.

Future Harvest

Nettle is a fast-growing perennial which thrives in moist ditches and along stream banks. Gather upper stalks, stems, and leaves but leave as much of the plant intact as possible for photosynthesis to ensure next year's growth.

oak

Quercus species

`EDIBLE` nut

Acorns are a quintessential forager's food. A few barrels of acorns gathered before winter will bring you an abundance of nutrient-dense carbohydrates and plant proteins. Once leached in a water bath, the acorn nutmeat is similar in flavor to the chestnut, and it can be used in soups and pulverized into nut butter, as well as ground into flour for baking.

How to Identify

White and red oaks (genus *Quercus*) are identifiable by their gray bark and alternate leaves, clustered at the terminal bud, each with soft, round edges. To discern between the two groups of oaks, white oaks have round-tipped leaves and red oaks have pointed leaves. Leaves can be deeply lobed or have no lobes at all. All acorns can have spiny or shaggy caps. Both the red and

Acorns ready for gathering—by squirrels or by foragers.

A Nutty Job: Processing Acorns

Shelling can be done tediously by hand, with a hammer or pair of pliers (squeeze twice to split open, says a friend forager) in front of a good TV show. I'd recommend investing in a hand-cranked nutcracker to process large batches, but they are expensive. Maybe your group of forager friends could invest in one together. Large pieces of nutmeats are easier to remove from the shell than crushed bits, so plan your smashing accordingly.

The acorn nutmeats will then need to be leached to remove the tannins from the nut and make it palatable. There are several methods for leaching, including a hot process and a cold process, each of which affects the final ground acorn product differently.

The hot water process will leech the tannins faster and can be done on a stovetop over the course of a long weekend. First, finely chop the nutmeats in a blender. This will increase the surface area of the nut that touches the water and thus speeds us the leech time.

Then, simmer the finely chopped nutmeats in water at a 1:5 ratio and replace the water until the nutmeats are palatable and nutty, not bitter. Acorns from white oaks are less tannic than the red and will have a shorter leaching process. The nutmeats, once leached, must be fully dried in a warm oven or dehydrator and then stored in a freezer immediately to prevent the acorn from going rancid if they aren't used immediately in cooking.

white oak produce acorns that are high in tannins, so they are not as palatable when fresh, but a good leaching can remedy the tannic flavor. White oaks have less tannin and produce the preferred acorn among foragers.

a winter's leaching and do not germinate until the spring (leaching helps to reduce their tannic flavor). The amount of the harvest will vary year to year: some seasons will bring bumper crops, and other years won't be as abundant.

Where and When to Gather

Both red and white oaks are well distributed across the Midwest. If you want to gather the acorns, it's advisable to head out harvesting later in the fall, as the first drops generally have the most insect damage. The acorns will fall in waves across the season, and they can be readily gathered off the ground well into the winter, particularly red acorns which benefit from

How to Gather

As you gather acorns, make sure to discard nuts with obvious insect infestation. Gather only those with firm, clean, and fresh-looking discs (the spot on top of the acorn where the cap was once affixed). Also discard any whose cap appears dislodged, moldy, or simply "off."

The shelf life for fresh acorns is terribly short, so they should be dried on a screen

White oak acorns still on the tree, not yet ready to be gathered.

Oaks in a local park can yield an abundance of acorns. While white oaks produce less-tannic acorns than reds, the red oak acorns can still be leached. Feel free to gather and try them for your own palate if there's a stand nearby to you.

or in a dehydrator or placed in dry, cold storage that stays below 50 degrees F, such as an unheated basement, if you want to save them. Check regularly for mold.

How to Eat

The leached nutmeats can be used whole, and toasting them brings out a nice roasted flavor similar to that of the chestnut. Acorns can be substituted in chestnut recipes, including as a finely ground flour that can be added to baking mixes. Remember that there is no gluten in acorn flour, so baking projects need to be planned accordingly.

Acorn flour is rich in carbohydrates and plant proteins. Stir the processed flour into smoothies to add wild nutrient density in lieu of commercial protein powders. The nutmeat can also be transformed into a nut butter or paste to add to other foraged flavors like chaga, chestnut, and hickory to create a tasty spread.

Future Harvest

Oaks are widespread across the Midwest and have not yet been threatened by the Sudden Oak Death disease seen in the West, but Oak Wilt is a concern in the Midwest. However, habitat loss is always an issue for our large hardwoods, although gathering the acorns will not significantly impact the propagation of smaller oaks.

ostrich fern

Matteuccia struthiopteris

EDIBLE fiddleheads

From late April and on into early May, the ostrich fern's small and coiled fiddlehead fronds push up through the soil and offer up one of spring's classic foraged foods. The fiddlehead can be cooked as a green vegetable for salads, pizza, pastas, and stir-fries.

How to Identify

The ancient-looking ostrich fern grows in dense colonies in woodland areas with rich, well-drained soils. About five to nine fronds per plant begin as fiddleheads in early spring, and each fiddlehead will have a brown, papery sheathing. The plant produces both sterile and fertile fronds. The sterile fronds are green and grow up to 36 inches tall, and the fertile fronds are smaller, brown, and unfurl in late summer.

Where and When to Gather

Seek out unfurled fiddleheads in late April and early May in the moist, rich soil found in mixed hardwood forests. The

Fiddleheads unfurling in early spring, at a good stage for harvesting.

Stems grow from the center crown. Note the brown papery sheathing over the fiddlehead, as well as the U-shaped indent or groove down the middle of the stem.

The remnants of last season's fertile frond are good ways to seek out unfurling fiddleheads in the early spring.

fiddleheads coincide with other delicious spring edibles including morels, spring beauties, trout lily, and wild leeks.

How to Gather

Using clippers, a sharp knife, or kitchen shears, gather only a few fiddleheads per fern to ensure the plant's viability later in the year. Once in the kitchen, wash the fiddleheads. Remove any brown sheathing from the plant. The fiddleheads can be stored in the refrigerator for up to a week. Compost any that turn soft or brown.

How to Eat

First, cook the fiddleheads in boiling water for at least 10 minutes to neutralize compounds that render them inedible when raw. Then the fiddleheads can be frozen for later use in the season. Failure to cook the fiddleheads in water first can cause stomach upset.

Fiddleheads will remain remarkably crunchy even after boiling, with a taste and texture similar to crunchy asparagus. They can be sautéed in butter and garlic, tossed into Italian pasta dishes, and are superb with cream sauces. Fiddleheads are also versatile in Asian dishes, with soy sauces.

Future Harvests

Habitat loss is a threat to the ostrich fern, as is overharvesting of this popular spring edible. Gather with a discerning eye and do not cut more than one or two fiddleheads from each crown.

ox-eye daisy

Leucanthemum vulgare

EDIBLE flowers, leaves

A common roadbank wildflower that spreads across the fields and meadows in June, the ox-eye daisy is a fun and yummy flower to forage, and it's one that will help introduce children to foraging as well.

How to Identify

Ox-eye daisy is a clumping perennial. In early spring, its basal rosette has long aromatic leaves that are ovate, toothed, and hairy. The plant sends up a flower stalk around summer solstice and blooms with a white disk flower that has petals arranged in a ray around a yellow center.

The ox-eye daisy dots meadows and road banks in June.

Where and When to Gather

The small, tender basal rosette leaves can be gathered in the spring. They become dry and rough later on in the season, particularly after the plant has gone to flower.

How to Gather

Pick the flower heads while in full bloom. Use fresh or preserve by drying the entire flower blossom on a screen. Store dried flowers in an airtight container to preserve freshness.

How to Eat

The leaves of the first-year plant's basal rosette can be picked and eaten raw in sandwiches or salads. They have a sweet, slightly astringent, carrot taste.

The ox-eye daisy is a fun flower to gather and add fresh to salads. They can be tossed with egg to make a flower fritter (add in other late spring greens and herbs to add substance to the fritter). Dredge the flowers in a tempura batter and fry in sesame oil to put atop a chilled rice noodle salad. The dried flowers can be added to a vegetable soup at the end of cooking for a showy garnish.

The aromatic and astringent leaves of the plant can be prepared as a hot tea (using dry or fresh leaves) which can be sipped to soothe allergies and a post nasal drip-like cough.

Future Harvests

The ox-eye daisy is a common wildflower, but it appears less and less as development of open fields and meadows cause habitat loss. The forager can propagate these flowers with seeds or transplants from the original colony of plants.

pawpaw
Asimina triloba

EDIBLE fruit

Pawpaw is known as the Midwest's false banana. Not only is this fruit similar to the banana in both texture and flavor, but it is also nutrient dense. Pawpaws freeze well, making them a worthy prize for the forager to seek out and preserve for the winter.

How to Identify

The tree has thin brown bark and grows to heights of 30 to 40 feet. Its leaves are 10 to 12 inches long, toothless, broad, oblong, and arranged alternately along the branches. When bruised, the leaf smells like used motor oil. It's frequently found alongside spicebush.

Pawpaw has two to eight maroon flowers in late spring. Their odor and color resemble rotten meat, which attracts pollinating flies. The fruit, hidden under the leaves, is

Pawpaw fruit ripe for eating.

The pawpaw tree has thin, gray-brown bark and grows to heights of 30 to 40 feet.

pale green like the undersides of the leaves, smooth skinned and hard. They have the skin color and hardness of a pear, but the size and shape of a short but thick cucumber. They soften and become fragrant when they are ripe.

The skin may become discolored with gray to black patches, but unlike with bananas, the discoloration does not necessarily indicate ripeness. Each fruit has a few 1- to 2-inch seeds. The flesh of the fruit starts out white, then it yellows when ripe and ready to eat.

Where and When to Gather

Pawpaw is found along stream banks and openings in the forests and in the understory of mixed hardwood forests in the central and southern areas of the Midwest. The fruit is normally ready to harvest in late September into October, depending on the season's weather. Wait to select pawpaw fruit that is no longer green, but more yellow and significantly soft to the touch.

How to Gather

Pawpaws can be green and still be ripe. The key is in the softness of the flesh—it should feel soft to the touch and will range in color from creamy white to yellow. The wind-fallen fruits are good bets, but as the fruit is perishable, you'll have to time your harvest with a fall wind or storm that helps shake the fruit off the tree.

The fruit ripens quickly once off the tree and on your kitchen counter, in only a few days (think browning banana). It will need to be stored or processed for later use. If the fruit is not prepared to be eaten fresh right away, wrap it in a cloth or paper bag, and it will keep for up to a week in the refrigerator, or the pulp can be scooped from the flesh (removing seeds) and frozen for later use in baking and smoothies.

How to Eat

The fruit can be eaten fresh or used frozen. As a fresh fruit, pawpaws can be peeled and sliced (remove seeds first) and served on a cheese plate with raw honey and locally harvested nuts. It pairs well with mints, cinnamon, and coconut flavors, and makes a nice addition to a fresh fruit salad.

The fruit pulp of the pawpaw can be mashed and cooked into tapioca or rice puddings. The fresh or frozen fruit pulp can be tossed into smoothies or used in baking for recipes that call for bananas like banana bread. The fruit pulp can also be churned into a delicious and rich ice cream.

Pawpaws are high in vitamin C, magnesium, iron, copper, manganese, and fatty acids. Pawpaws also contain potassium, calcium, amino acids, and antioxidants.

Future Harvests

You can help grow an abundance of pawpaw by working with local growers of the domestic plant (who will be familiar with the genetic breeding needs of the pawpaw) to add it into landscaping of local parks. For the permaculturist, the pawpaw is an excellent addition to a woodland garden and wild wood spaces.

pennycress

Thalpsi arvense

`EDIBLE` leaves, seeds

Pennycress offers garlicky spring greens as well as its mustard seeds, which can be used as an aromatic culinary spice in the kitchen.

How to Identify

Pennycress is a biennial plant that produces a basal rosette in its first year and grows erect and tall, up to 2 feet in height. Its leaves have a garlic-like odor. They are alternate, oblong, and slightly lobed.

In its second year, pennycress produces clusters of white flowers in late spring. Heart-shaped seedpods produce small, aromatic, brownish-black mustard seeds useful as a culinary spice.

Pennycress in flower. Its leaves are garlicky in flavor, similar to that of garlic mustard.

Pennycress seeds can be used similarly to mustard seeds as a culinary spice.

Where and When to Gather
Pennycress is a wild weed, abundant in open fields and empty lots with rocky, disturbed soil. The small, new greens should be gathered in early spring and the heart-shaped seedpods of the second-year plants collected in late summer. The greens and stems become tough and bitter when the plant goes to flower.

How to Gather
Gather the small, tender leaves by hand for use in the kitchen. To use and preserve the seeds, winnow the papery husk from the seed and store in a airtight container.

How to Eat
Pennycress has a strong garlic-mustard flavor. When young, tender, and small, the aromatic greens can be sautéed for egg dishes like frittatas, or added to stir-fries. The dry seeds can be used in place of store-bought mustard seeds. Use pennycress seeds to make a foraged stone-ground mustard or vinaigrette dressing.

Future Harvests
Like other mustard family plants, pennycress is self-sowing and reproduces rapidly in areas of disturbed soil. It qualifies as a weed in some places. In others areas, though, pennycress is being field-tested as a potential biofuel source. Harvesting pennycress from the wild will not impact its future harvests.

peppermint

Mentha piperita

EDIBLE leaves

There's nothing quite like the power of fresh peppermint in a spring salad or in a refreshing iced tea or cocktail. Peppermint is a common wild herb and a staple herb for any kitchen.

Peppermint is a must-have for every kitchen. It's great fresh in mojitos and is essential dried as tea for the apothecary.

How to Identify

Peppermint is a creeping perennial that grows to heights of 2 feet. It has durable square stems, ranging in color from green to red to brown, depending on its cultivar. Its leaves are opposite, lance-shaped, and toothed. It produces small, white to pale purple flower heads in early summer, after which the plant dries significantly and begins to die back.

Where and When to Gather

Peppermint is a widely growing plant that prefers moist, well-drained soil along stream banks in partial sun. It is tender and more aromatic in mid-spring, and then becomes rougher and spicier as the weather warms and before it goes to flower, when it becomes significantly drier. Peppermint will return in the later fall when the weather cools.

How to Gather

Collect the plant before flowering for the choicest leaves and best flavor. But note that it can be gathered and used anytime across the season; just use your nose and tastebuds to determine the flavor and quality.

Full stems of peppermint can be gathered, bundled, and dried for tea, or the plant can be used fresh in the kitchen. The herb stores for up to a week fresh wrapped in a moist tea towel in the refrigerator, but for maximum aroma, process the plant immediately upon harvesting.

How to Eat

Freshly foraged peppermint can be used in as many ways as its cultivated counterpart (which is really equally wild). There's nothing simpler than a peppermint aqua fresca, mojito, or Moscow Mule on a warm spring afternoon on the patio after a hard session in the garden.

Toss the fresh peppermint into savory green salads, chilled bean salads, pasta salads, and rice dishes. Freshly found mint is a wonderful addition to newly dug potatoes and spring peas, or wild asparagus and cattail shoots. For the main entree, fresh peppermint can be used to flavor mint sauces for fish and lamb.

Turn fresh peppermint into a simple syrup for the cocktail cart, and use it in mixed drinks or for baking projects—or even to flavor peppermint ice cream. Dry the foraged peppermint for tea. One or two armful-sized bundles can make enough tea for a family of four for winter's use. Dry peppermint is an invaluable herbal remedy to soothe upset stomachs (small sips only). The tea is soothing, and peppermint's aroma can help shoo away winter malaise.

Future Harvest

Peppermint spreads voraciously via its underground runners, and gathering its long stalks will do little to affect the plant's future growth and harvest.

pineapple weed
Matricaria discoidea

EDIBLE flowers, leaves

Pineapple weed is a small and common plant with an aromatic flavor similar to a citrusy pineapple. The fresh leaves of pineapple weed can be added to a spring herbed salad or chopped fresh to season grilled white fish with lemon. Blended with other herbs, it can make a refreshing afternoon tea.

Pineapple weed is a scrubby plant that has flavors similar to those of top aromatic notes of chamomile and can be used as both a culinary herb and refreshing tea.

How to Identify

Pineapple weed is a funny name for a small, scrubby annual plant that grows nearly everywhere in poor-quality, disturbed soil. Take a moment to stoop down and crush the cone-shaped flower heads: it smells distinctively of pineapple and the sweeter notes of its relative, German chamomile *(Matricaria recutita)*. Usually, the plant only grows to about 6 inches tall, but it can get a bit larger, sometimes over a foot in bloom. Its feathery, dissected leaves are similar to those of chamomile, and its flowers are shallow, green-yellow cones.

Where and When to Gather

Pineapple weed grows most commonly in waste places—rocky soil, driveways, open fields, and empty lots. It is most flavorful and aromatic in the mid- to early spring and then again in the fall. Pineapple weed goes to flower in late spring, and then both the leaves and flowers can be enjoyed at the height of their aromatics. In the heat of the later summer, the plant dries back and the leaves and flower are more markedly bitter.

How to Gather

Harvest the leaves and flowers by hand or with kitchen scissors, taking care to choose sections that aren't too sandy as the plant is hard to clean. Pineapple weed can be used fresh, or it can be dried on a screen or in the dehydrator for later use.

How to Eat

The top notes of pineapple weed are sweet and very similar to pineapple. It is also slightly citrusy, making it a nice herb to use on light fishes or fresh cheeses. It can also be chopped fresh and added to an herbed salad.

Pineapple weed makes a fragrant iced tea when brewed with cool water (hot water will cause the bitterness of the plant to be the primary flavor). Brew the leaves and flowers in cold water along with lemon balm, catnip, rose petals, and mint. It is refreshing and stress-relieving on those warmer spring days. Brewing pineapple-weed in hot water for tea brings forward its bitterness significantly, and this can be helpful for upset stomachs, frazzled nerves, and even teething babies (pineapple weed popsicles, sweetened with honey, are perfect for them).

Future Harvests

Pineapple weed is considered by many to be just a weed with little value. Clipping the green tops of the plant will not hurt it at all, as it is resilient and easily reproduces.

plantain

Plantago species

`EDIBLE` leaves, seeds

Plantain is a perennial wild plant that reseeds easily and grows everywhere. In the early spring, plantain's small, tender, lemony leaves can be added into a wild salad greens mix.

Plantain is an abundant wild weed, growing in open spaces, sidewalks, and grassy fields.

How to Identify

Plantain grows as a basal rosette, with either broad or narrow leaves, depending on the species. The foliage of broadleaf plantain is smooth and veined, growing up to 6 inches long and 4 inches wide. The leaf stems are fibrous and can have a red tinge at the base. The foliage of the narrow leaf plantain is slightly more dry and hairy, with long leaves up to 6 to 8 inches that are lance-shaped and pointed. Both species produce long flower stalks in midsummer covered with small white blossoms that give way to small edible seeds commonly seen in health food shops as psyllium husks.

Where and When to Gather

Plantain grows abundantly in fields and waste places. It is a weed that lives where people live: look for it in parks, in cracks in the sidewalk, and on the trail. Don't gather plantain where dogs may stop along the trail, as it seems to like to grow in often-visited spots.

How to Gather

Gather the fresh leaves in spring while they are vibrant and fresh. Plantain, however, is abundant almost everywhere and can be harvested across the season. Harvest the dry brown seeds in late summer, winnow them from the flower stalk, and store them in an airtight container.

How to Eat

In salads, raw young plantain leaves add a lemony flavor. Plantain also makes a nice wild tea that can be helpful in combination with slippery elm or marshmallow root, along with a dollop of raw, local honey, to help soothe a dry, raspy cough. Plantain seeds, also called psyllium seeds, are useful as a binder ingredient in gluten-free baking, and because of its mucilaginous, expansive quality, it can be added to smoothies and is good for anyone who wants to add a healing fiber to his or her diet.

Future Harvests

Plantain reseeds easily, so you can harvest it safely without significant worry of impacting the future sustainability of the plant.

poke

Phytolacca americana

pokeweed

`EDIBLE` shoots

Only the very young shoots of poke are edible, but their neutral flavor makes them a versatile vegetable in egg dishes and stir-fries, or a nice side dish of cooked greens.

How to Identify

Shoots emerge in mid-spring, but poke grows to heights of 6 to 8 feet, with robust tubular stalks that when mature can have bright pink striping along the stalk. Its overall color is a vibrant green, with a smooth and waxy texture. Its leaves are alternate, long, smooth, and wavy. The small whitish-green flower clusters bloom in early summer and develop drooping clusters of beautiful dark purple berries in late summer. The stalk and the leaf stems become magenta-colored as the season progresses.

Here, poke shoots are emerging adjacent to a stalk from last season. They can be gathered until they grow to no more than 6 inches, as larger plants have concentrated compounds that may make an eater sick.

Where and When to Gather

The only safe, edible portions of poke are the new shoots in mid-spring. Poke loves a wide range of poor-quality soils, from acidic, sandy soils to heavy clay. It is commonly found in disturbed ground and in waste places alongside burdock and various evergreens. The perennial plant pushes up through the ground in mid-spring, flowers in early summer, and develops berries in late July and into August.

How to Gather

Collect only green spring shoots that are under 6 inches in height, making sure the stems haven't begun to branch or leaf out, are free of any vibrant pink along the stalk, and have not gone to flower. The new shoots can be trimmed with scissors, then cleaned and parboiled before preparing. The parboiled shoots can be frozen in zipper bags for later use.

How to Eat

Enjoy tender poke shoots by boiling, changing the salted water several times to remove any potential alkaloid toxins. The flavors of the greens are relatively neutral, and once cooked, poke greens can be prepared as you would asparagus shoots. Cooked poke shoots can be drizzled with olive oil, sea salt, and lemon, and then topped with the chopped, fresh green tops of the wild leek. The shoots can also make a delicious side dish topped with cheeses, hollandaise sauce, or a wild garlic mustard pesto.

Future Harvests

Poke is a common wild plant. Harvesting its early shoots to eat or berries for ink will do little to impact its future plant population.

Caution

Mature pokeweed is inedible and in some cases can cause sickness. Harvest only the early poke shoots that are free of the vibrant pink. The shoots should be no more than 6 inches tall, without flowers and branches along the stalk.

prickly pear

Opuntia species

nopales

`EDIBLE` fruits, pads

Cactus in the Midwest, you ask? Yes! From grilled nopales pads to nopales smoothies and prickly pear margaritas, the prickly pear is an excellent foraged food that offers both its pads and its fruit for foraging.

Cactus does grow in the Midwest—and it's edible as well.

Tender prickly pear paddles are good for harvesting right before going into bloom.

How to Identify

Prickly pear is a low-growing or climbing perennial plant, with large 6- to 8-inch pad-like leaves. It has large spines growing out of the pads and fruits, as well as tiny spines called glochids. The flowers of the prickly pear bloom in early summer and range in color from yellow to red. These produce succulent pinkish-red fruits (also known as *tunas*) that can be harvested through the fall. The entire plant shrivels and dries back at the end of fall, after the first frosts.

Where and When to Gather

The prickly pear grows in colonies, spreading across disturbed sandy and rocky soils, in south-facing, sunny locations. It is commonly cultivated as a landscape plant. Harvest the pads across the growing season, choosing those that are green and firm-fleshed. Gather the fruits when they are bright and succulent looking, before the plant begins to die back in the late fall.

How to Gather

Both the prickly pear pads and fruits are covered in large and tiny spines. While the large spines are somewhat avoidable, the glochids (the smaller spines) are pesky buggers that can get into the skin and feel like a fiberglass rash. The glochids will embed themselves into fabric, so do your gathering with leather gloves and harvest

Prickly pear fruits, or tunas, are flavorful and make a delicious simple syrup for margaritas.

directly into a paper bag that can be discarded (the tiny spines are hard to remove from a fabric harvest bag, ruining it for re-use later) or a solid-surface bowl.

In the kitchen, prepare the pads and the fruits with gloves. To remove the glochids, hold the pad or fruit with tongs and torch them first over an open flame. Once the spines are burnt off, the prickly pear can be peeled, chopped, or pureed as the recipes requires.

How to Eat

Prickly pear pads have a firm but fleshy texture with a fresh green flavor similar to a honeydew melon. The peeled pads can be chopped and used for a fresh fruit smoothie, or combined with black beans, corn, garlic, and cilantro for a refreshing nopales salad. The pads can also be cooked into egg dishes, grilled or roasted for casseroles, or served over wild rice.

The prickly pear fruit has a sweet watermelon-bubble-gummy scent and flavor. Once de-needled, it can be pureed and run through a food mill or strainer to remove seeds. Then the puree can be made into a simple syrup for margaritas, or the puree can be made into a frozen fruit sherbet or dessert topping. The puree and syrup can also be made into a barbecue glaze for pork, chicken, or tofu.

Future Harvests

The prickly pear can be propagated by cuttings. It grows easily in disturbed, rocky, and sandy soils, and is cold tolerant. Plant in south-facing areas for most prolific growth.

purslane
Portulaca oleracea

EDIBLE leaves, stems, flowers, seeds

Raw or cooked purslane has a fresh, distinctly lemon-sour note. It's high in protein and omega-3 essential fatty acids (take note, vegetarian friends) as well as life-sustaining minerals such as calcium, magnesium, copper, and manganese.

How to Identify

Purslane is found everywhere: fields, garden beds, gravel parking lots, and sidewalk cracks. It pops up nearly anywhere between June and August. It's easy to identify, with its round, fleshy, reddish stems. Purslane leaves are smooth and shiny, dark green, thick, paddle-like, and rounded; they grow in an alternate, nearly opposite pattern along the stem.

When the leaves and stems are crushed, you can tell that it's a juicy plant. The juice should be clear and watery—not a milky sap, which is one way to distinguish it from

Purslane is a nutritious, flavorful, and succulent green that grows abundantly as a weed in gardens, flower beds, and disturbed soils across the Midwest.

prostrate spurge (*Euphorbia maculata*, a creeping, inedible plant in the same habitat as purslane).

Purslane's leaves cluster toward the apex of the stems with a tiny yellow flower that opens only in the morning. The flower features five yellow petals, two green sepals, and several stamens and pistils. The succulent leaves grow to about ½ to 1-inch long. The stems can be as thick as a pencil and curl upward at the end, and they can reach 6 to 8 inches above the ground if the soil is rich. Conversely, they will be smaller and scraggly looking in poor soil.

Where and When to Gather
In midsummer, this sprawling succulent is found in well-drained soils of gardens and lawns, usually in areas that have been well-tilled and receive moderate to full sun exposure. It is also resilient enough to be found growing between the sidewalk cracks. Look around—it really is everywhere! It puts out many seeds and can reproduce easily.

How to Gather
The edible parts of purslane are the leaves, stems, flowers, and seeds. Gather clean, spot-free stems and leaf tops. Wait until the plant has stems of reasonable size to yield enough for a meal, and clip only the tops so the plant will re-sprout, leaving you with a productive plant for the duration of the summer months.

How to Eat
The leafy and succulent edible purslane tops are a versatile vegetable. Purslane is similar to bean sprouts in texture and lemony in flavor. It shines in a variety of Asian dishes, like a Thai coconut soup, a spicy Indian curry pad Thai, or a hot bowl of pho, or gumbo. Purslane makes a great addition to a stir-fry. Be sure to add the purslane at the end of the cooking time so as not to overcook the green.

Purslane can shine on its own as a salad, chopped and tossed with a simple lemon vinaigrette dressing with a dash of salt and pepper. It can even be added to Asian slaws (cabbage, kohlrabi, even shredded beet slaws) and used in place of bean sprouts in spring rolls. It also preserves well as a pickle.

Future Harvests
Purslane is a common garden weed, appearing nearly every summer in garden spaces and waste places in the soil. Harvesting the tops of the plant will do little to affect future harvests.

raspberry

Rubus idaeus, R. occidentalis

EDIBLE berries, leaves, root

Raspberries—both red and black—are a favorite summer fruit. Whether enjoyed by the handful trailside while walking to the beach or gathered for a summer fruit pie, the raspberry is easy to identify and a must-gather for the forager.

How to Identify

The thorny canes of red (*Rubus idaeus*) and black (*Rubus occidentalis*) raspberry are sprawling and grow in large stands at the edges of the woodlands. The leaves are toothed with pointed ends, grow alternately in leaflets of three to five along the canes, and are green with a silvery underside. Raspberry flowers in late spring. Black raspberries ripen in midsummer, while red raspberries ripen in late summer to early fall.

Where and When to Gather

The raspberry is a native woodland plant found at the edges of the woods, trails,

Ripe red raspberries are a thirst-quenching delight to gather while walking the trails in late summer.

Black raspberries ripen earlier than the red, and the leaves can be used similarly.

hedgerows, and ditches. The leaves can be gathered for tea in early spring and late fall.

How to Gather

Pick the ripe fruits of the black raspberry in early July and the red raspberry in August to early September. They can be used right away or frozen for later. Gather in the summer sun when sugars in the berries are highest and the fruit is most sweet.

Gather the leaves in the early spring before the plant begins to develop flowers, usually in early June. The leaves can also be gathered again in the late fall after the plant is done fruiting. If you are thinning a stand of raspberry canes, the entire cane can be pruned and stripped of its leaves. The leaves can be used fresh or dried on a screen. The root can be dug anytime for use as a tea, but this is easiest in fall or spring when you are thinning the canes.

How to Eat

Crumbles, pie, bars, jam, fruit leather, ice cream, and more: there are so many ways to use raspberries. The berries can be fermented to make wine or turned into a simple syrup for cocktails and cordials. Crushed raspberries, macerated with raw apple cider vinegar, can be infused for several days, strained, and served cold for a refreshing and nutritious raspberry vinegar shrub.

As the fruits of the raspberry freeze well for winter's use, be sure to put some up for a real treat when snow blankets the ground. There's nothing like whipping up a batch of jam or a homemade pie made with delicious summer fruit.

Raspberry leaves are known for their vitamin C and rich mineral content. Blend them with other herbs like red clover, nettle, and oat straw, then boil the mix to create a beverage high in calcium, magnesium, silica, and other minerals. Add in foraged mushrooms like maitake, reishi, and turkey tail, and you can create a delicious, nutrient-dense vegan broth base for soups and stews.

Future Harvests

The raspberry can be propagated easily with cuttings or by transplanting the canes. They spread quickly and are tolerant of a lazy gardener. You can trellis the canes or let them grow as they will along a woodland edge as part of a permaculture landscape plan. As the raspberry is a voracious perennial spreader, gathering the leaves and fruits of the plant will have a minimal impact on future harvests.

redbud

Cercis canadensis

EDIBLE flowers, leaves, seed pods

As the snow melts and the trees begin to unfurl their leaves, you can gather the redbud's early tender leaves and showy purple flowers to enjoy raw or cooked. Later in the summer, you can eat the seedpods, too.

The redbud leaf is easily recognizable by its smooth-edged, heart-shaped form. Early tender leaves of the redbud can be enjoyed in salads.

Redbud flowers are not only beautiful but also edible. Feature them in salads or even pickle the unopened buds for a tasty culinary garnish that is similar in taste and texture to capers.

How to Identify

Redbud is a small but graceful tree, growing only to heights of about 20 to 25 feet. It has smooth charcoal-gray bark and graceful branches with alternate, heart-shaped green leaves. The blossoms form in clusters along the branches in early spring. From these, 3- to 4-inch-long flat seedpods develop.

Where and When to Gather

Redbud grows along the edges of the woods. It is a beautiful tree and is often used as a landscaping ornamental, but it also grows wild and in abundance across the Midwest. You can harvest from it in spring and summer.

How to Gather

Redbud leaves are choice when they first unfurl in the early spring. Gather them when they are still soft and tender to the touch. Both flower buds and flowers can be gathered, but if you want to gather the seedpods later, leave sufficient flowers on the branches to produce the pods. Gather

Enjoy tender, newly formed redbud pods in recipes that call for snow peas.

the pods in early summer while they are still green and tender. The seedpods will become more dry and chewy as the season progresses.

How to Eat

Redbud's tender green leaves have a slightly sour but mostly neutral flavor. They can be chopped raw into salads or lightly steamed. The unopened flower buds can be pickled in a vinegar brine to make a colorful pickle that has a caper-like texture and can be used as such.

The opened buds make a delightful garnish for a foraged spring salad. The flowers also can withstand cooking and can be added to a fritter or put atop an egg scramble. Older buds will begin to develop an acrid taste, so pick early. The early green seedpods have a flavor and texture similar to fresh green peas and are best when 1 to 2 inches long and greenish pink. Sauté, steam, or fry the pods.

Future Harvests

Redbud produces saplings easily with its abundance of seedpods. Take this into consideration when gathering the buds and flowers, especially if you want to cultivate a large stand of redbuds (which make a striking spring landscape visual). Redbud is an excellent tree to incorporate into a permaculture landscape plan as it is both visually striking and edible.

red clover

Trifolium praetense

EDIBLE flowers, leaves

Dotting open fields and spaces with its red blossoms, red clover is a brightly flavored, nutritious weed that you can gather in abundance and add to teas and soups to boost nutritional content.

How to Identify

Red clover is a low-growing plant that can cover the ground, but it can also stand as tall as 2 feet. The plant has three soft leaflets per stem, and the leaves are arranged alternately along the stem. The stem is hairy. Red clover begins to blossom in June, featuring a showy reddish-pink bloom head comprising many small, nectar-filled, tubular florets.

Red clover is a common lawn weed that can be gathered in abundance in fields that have not been mowed and at the edges of mowed lawns. It has branched, hairy stems with several red flower heads per plant.

Where and When to Gather

Red clover grows abundantly in sunny, open spaces and can tolerate both moist and dry soil. It begins to bloom around the solstice and remains in bloom throughout the summer.

How to Gather

Gather the blossoms and top greens by hand or with scissors on a dry, sunny day. Choose only the flowers that are vibrant and free of brown withering. Do not gather blossoms that are damp or wet as they will wilt or could mold while drying. The blossoms can be used fresh or easily dried on screens for later use. Because red clover is high in mineral content, harvest only in areas that are free from pesticides, nitrate pollution, and heavy metal contamination.

How to Eat

Clover blossoms and greens are mineral-rich and contain calcium, potassium, and magnesium, among other nutrients. The blossoms can be eaten fresh: they have a green taste, but can be a bit dry to incorporate into a salad. The fresh blossoms do work well in a greens fritter, egg dish, or in soups and have a flavor similar to the sweet pea. They can also be steamed and used as garnish or side dish with a light white fish or chicken.

To fully extract the clover's mineral density, extract fresh or dry plant material in a long infusion of hot water, or boil for 20 minutes. The red clover extraction mixes well in an infusion with nettle, oat straw, horsetail, or raspberry to make a nutrient-dense beverage which can be enjoyed as an iced or room-temperature tea, or added to smoothies, soups, or stews. It can also be used to soak beans, lentils, or rice, or you can cook pasta in it to infuse those carbohydrates with additional nutrition.

Future Harvests

Red clover is an abundant edible wild plant. As it is a perennial, it comes back easily after being gathered or even mowed. Gathering the blossoms and green tops will not affect future harvests.

Caution

There has been some debate over clover's possible effects on hormone balance, but traditional use suggests it is safe for general consumption as a nutritious food.

rose

Rosa species

`EDIBLE` buds, flowers, hips

The heady perfume of the rose rests on the summer breezes of June, guiding you to brambles filled with blossoms and unopened buds ready to be gathered by the basketful and infused into cocktails, beverages, pastries, confections, and savory dishes.

How to Identify

Rose is a spreading shrub that grows to be about 5 feet tall. Its canes are thorny and have alternate, finely serrated compound leaves that are deep green and shiny. The rosebuds form in mid-June and then open

Wild roses are abundant across the Midwest. Their petals and hips can be used as culinary herbs in many drinks and dishes.

into blooms that are five-petaled and range in color from white to dark pink, from 1 to 3 inches in diameter, depending on the species. After the rose is pollinated, it forms its fruit, called rose hips, in late summer. These range in size from ¼ to 1½ inches in diameter. The hips will turn dark red after the first hard frost.

Where and When to Gather

Wild roses love disturbed rocky soil, woodland edges, and locations near lakes and rivers. Gather the unopened buds and petals in early summer. Rose hips are best gathered in late fall after the frost when their flavors are more pronounced.

Rose hips are high in vitamin C and can be collected and preserved after the frost in the fall.

How to Gather

Gather unopened buds and flowers using pruners or scissors and dry them flat on screens. Harvest on a dry, sunny day. Wet weather will diminish the aromatics and make the plant material very fragile. Gather from healthy plants; roses are frequently susceptible to mildew, blight, and aphids. The rose hips will be orange until a frost, when they turn a dark, bright red. On the larger rose hips, scoop out the seeds and the interior if possible before drying or cooking, to avoid possible stomach upset.

How to Eat

Use wild rose petals to make a rosewater hydrosol or rose simple syrup. The rosewater and simple syrup can be used to flavor shortbreads, biscotti, cakes, and poached fruits. The rose simple syrup can flavor ice cream, plain yogurt, sorbet, panna cotta, and meringue, as well as vodka punch, champagne, non-alcoholic sodas, and sparkling water.

Candy the rose petals and rosebuds to dress up desserts and other confections. For beverages, rose petals can be infused into tequila and vodkas for rose liquors and cordials. Citrusy flavored wild rose hips are high in vitamin C. Add dried or fresh hips to cordials, jelly, and syrups.

Future Harvests

The wild rose is deemed a noxious weed in some areas. It can be easily propagated by canes, and gathering its buds, petals, and hips will not significantly impact future harvests.

salsify

Tragopogon species

goat's beard

`EDIBLE` flowers, leaves, roots, stems

Salsify is known for its large, showy, dandelion-like flower and oversized, fluffy seed head. It's a versatile plant that, like the dandelion, offers nutritious edible spring greens and roots for your harvest.

A salsify flower head gone to seed is an easy way to locate and identify this plant. The seed head is slightly spherical and resembles a giant dandelion seed head.

How to Identify

Salsify is a biennial plant that grows in a variety of disturbed waste places and open fields. The leaves are long, narrow, and alternate, and they appear in early spring. From the leaves, a tall, hollow stem grows which exudes a white, milky sap when cut.

The 2- to 3-inch salsify flower is a brilliant yellow array of petals, similar to the dandelion in appearance, but larger and with green bracts beneath the blooms. The flower develops into a dramatic seed head with fluffy tufts at the end of the seeds that look similar to a goat's beard (hence the name). The root is relatively spindly, thin, and white.

Salsify's flowers, leaves, and stems can be used as cooked greens in frittatas or similar dishes.

Where, and When to Gather

Salsify grows in open fields of rocky soil and disturbed waste places. In early spring, salsify greens can be gathered for spring greens. The leaves become more bitter, dry, and tough with warmer weather, so take this into consideration when gathering.

How to Gather

The root can be dug, cleaned and used immediately, or it can be chopped, dried, and roasted for later use as a tea. Leaves, stems, and flowers can be gathered in spring and summer.

How to Eat

Salsify's leaves, stems, and flowers can all be added to a spring or summer salad, as long as it's early in the season. However, later season and more bitter pickings can be cooked in a stir-fry or in butter for a frittata or other similar dish and still be quite palatable.

The roots taste sweet like parsnip, but are quite spindly. Boil and then combine them with other tubers, rhizomes, and roots for a dish of much substance. Its texture holds up well as a fermented pickle and results in a crunchy root perfect as a garnish.

Future Harvests

Salsify is deemed an invasive weed across much of the Midwest, particularly in the western half. It's resilient and easily self-propagates. Gathering the plant will not significantly harm its future harvest.

sassafras

Sassafras albidum

EDIBLE bark, leaves, roots

A taste of sassafras leaves in the heat of the summer sun will give you a sweet, cooling bite of the plant's aromatic flavor. Its leaves can be used as a thickening agent in cooking, while its aromatic roots can improve chai and other beverages with their spicy flavor.

How to Identify

Sassafras is a small deciduous tree that grows to heights of up to 60 feet or more in optimum conditions. Its bark is a rough and reddish brown, and its leaves are alternate, smooth, and soft; some are ovate with no lobe, others are mitten-shaped, and still others have three lobes.

There are both male and female trees. The female flowers have no sepals and bear blue, oval fruit in late summer. The aromatic roots range in color from white to reddish brown. In fact, the entire plant is aromatic, with a scent that is reminiscent of spicy root beer or fruit-flavored cereal.

Where and When to Gather

Sassafras loves sandy, well-drained soil and is found along the edges of fence lines, roadsides, beaches, orchards, and woodlands in partial sun. Leaves can be harvested anytime, although the young leaves in the first part of the season are more tender, aromatic, and cooling. Later in the season, leaves are more dry.

How to Gather

Gather the leaves and dry them flat on a screen. Store in an airtight container. The roots of a small sapling can be gathered in the spring or fall. Wash, chop, and completely dry them. The bark can also be gathered from small branches in the spring.

How to Use

Sassafras leaves make a nice trail snack as the flavors are refreshing, perfect in the dry heat of summer. They can also be made into a cooling, soothing tea that is perfect iced. Rose petals, linden flowers, violet leaves and flowers, or lemon balm all work well combined with sassafras leaves for tea. The leaves are mucilaginous and slimy when wet and can be used in place of okra to thicken soups like gumbo.

The roots are more aromatic, drying, and more spicy than the leaves. They can work well in an aromatic chai with burdock, sarsaparilla, wild ginger, and spicebush. The bark can be used as an aromatic bitter similar to aspen.

Sassafras is common along trails and beach areas, and makes a delightful tea and culinary spice. It commonly has mitten-shaped, three-lobed, and un-lobed leaves.

Future Harvests

Sassafras is abundant and easily propagated by cuttings, seedlings, or suckers. You can gather handfuls of leaves from medium-sized trees without harming the plant. Gather the roots and branches from saplings.

serviceberry

Amelanchier species
saskatoon berry, juneberry

EDIBLE berries

With its perfectly balanced, sweet fruit, serviceberry is a delightful June find. Its berries are easy to gather and abundant, and they make delicious pies and jams—that is, if any make it home without being eaten. Quite possibly, this is one of my summer favorites.

How to Identify
Serviceberry is a small, fruiting, deciduous shrub or small tree that grows to a height of 20 feet. Its bark is smooth gray with dark vertical furrows. The leaves are oval, serrated, smooth or slightly hairy, and alternate along the stem. The white, five-petaled flowers bloom in early spring, and dark purple fruit in racemes ripens in midsummer. Each fruit has a small crown at the base, similar to an apple or pear.

Where and When to Gather
Serviceberry is found in the wild along hedgerows and in open woodlands. It is a common landscape plant whose fruits usually go unnoticed. The berries ripen in mid- to late June.

Serviceberries ripening on the bush in late June.

Serviceberries ready to be made into jam and pie—a delicious early summer harvest.

How to Gather

Harvest when the crop on the tree is mostly ripe and dark red, leaving the green fruit for later harvests over subsequent weeks. Bring baskets and gather by hand in the morning on a clear, dry day. A few pints can be easily gathered in a half hour or so. Before preserving, make sure the fruit is dry and clean of debris.

How to Eat

Serviceberry makes a nice jam, fruit leather, and, of course, pie. If the harvest is small, the berries can be mixed with other seasonal foraged fruits like blackberry, blueberry, or raspberry for baking, ice cream, cordials, and jams.

The fruit, with its mild flavor like a cross between a cherry and a blueberry, is a lovely complement to fresh farm cheese, yogurt, or ice cream. Like the huckleberry, serviceberries are excellent in milkshakes. Herbs like basil or lemon verbena pair well with serviceberry. It can also be combined in simple syrup for cocktails with a tequila or vodka, or simply to flavor a refreshing homemade soda.

Future Harvests

Serviceberry is a widely distributed plant that is also common in the landscape industry. Because of its appealing fruits, it is also becoming more popular as an early summer crop on farms in the northern areas of the Midwest. Harvesting the fruit will do little to impact the plant's future harvest or distribution across the Midwest. It propagates easily by cuttings and bare-root transplants, and it tolerates a variety of temperatures and soil conditions. Serviceberry makes for an excellent edible plant addition to a permaculture landscape design.

Solomon's seal

Polygonatum biflorum

EDIBLE rhizomes, shoots

Solomon's seal, a native woodland plant, offers you its early shoots and rhizomes as nutritious spring wild edibles. The early shoots taste like the new shoots of asparagus and the rhizomes like a sweet root vegetable.

Solomon's seal shoots at a good stage for harvesting.

Solomon's seal with unripe green fruit in summer.

The rhizome of false Solomon's seal's (*Maianthemum racemosum*) is edible and can be used like that of true Solomon's seal.

How to Identify

Solomon's seal grows to about 2 feet in height. Its stalk is erect and droops gracefully with the weight of its leaves and berries in the summertime. The leaves are green, smooth, veined, alternate, and in some species, slightly hairy. Its flowers develop beneath each leaf axil and produce 1/2 inch round berries that range in color from green to black.

The rhizome is thin, about 1/2 to 3/4 inch in diameter, white, and knobby. The plant is easy to identify in winter, as its stalks are sturdy and often there will be berries left for easy identification. It is a favorite for deer to munch on, especially in urban areas where there is little open space for them to roam and gather food.

False Solomon's seal (*Maianthemum racemosum*) is frequently mistaken for true Solomon's seal (*Polygonatum biflorum*) because of the similar erect, branching stalks and alternate leaves. A differentiating factor is the flower arrangement. False Solomon's seal has a white terminal flower plume at the end of the stem that produces bright red berries in midsummer.

True Solomon's seal has small, white blossoms that hang down from the leaf axils. These produce berries that range in color from green to black in midsummer. The roots of false Solomon's seal are also edible and can be used like those of the true Solomon's seal.

Where and When to Gather

Solomon's seal loves woodland shade. In some areas it grows abundantly in large stands and can carpet the ground. The new spring shoots can be gathered when they emerge in early spring. Once the shoots are up, or if you can find a stalk from last year, it is easy to locate and sustainably harvest the rhizome, which can then be gathered anytime.

Solomon's seal rhizomes have been harvested in the fall.

How to Gather

Use kitchen scissors to clip the early greens when they are up to 6 inches tall, when the leaves begin to unfurl. To sustainably gather the rhizomes, locate two adjacent stems of the plant, and seek out (with a small fork or digging tool) the connecting rhizome segment. Slice off the middle segment between the plants, taking care to leave sufficient rhizome so that the main stalk may remain intact and rooted beneath the soil. Wash the root well before eating or preparing.

How to Eat

The early shoots of Solomon's seal are tasty sautéed or simply grilled and drizzled with butter, salt, and lemon. The rhizomes have a crispy, nutty, sweet flavor, similar to a cross between a carrot and a parsnip. They can be boiled or cooked in butter. A less-known use of Solomon's seal is as a field medicine and herbal apothecary staple for musculoskeletal injuries and joint pain.

Future Harvests

Gathering the early spring shoots for food is the most sustainable way to eat Solomon's seal. The rhizomes are delicious, but preparing a full meal of Solomon's seal rhizomes on a regular basis could very well put a strain on the plant's population (even if only the middle rhizomes are gathered). The plant can be propagated by root cuttings and is a nice addition to a permaculture landscape plan.

spearmint

Mentha spicata

`EDIBLE` leaves

Freshly foraged spearmint can be used in as many ways as its cultivated counterpart. There's nothing more simple and delicious than a spearmint and lemon balm iced tea on a warm spring afternoon after a long walk in the woods.

How to Identify

Spearmint is a creeping perennial that grows to heights of 4 to 5 feet, but is best gathered when it is 1 to 3 feet tall. It has durable square stems with green, lance-shaped, toothed leaves growing opposite from one another and sessile (attached directly to the stem without a petiole). Each pair of leaves is at 90 degrees to the pair below and above it.

Spearmint is commonly found near stream banks and creek beds. It makes a wonderful culinary spice and tea.

It produces small and white, pale violet, or pink flower heads in late summer, after which the plant dries significantly and begins to die back.

Where and When to Gather

Like peppermint, spearmint grows wild in moist, well-drained soil along stream banks and in partial sun. It is tender and more aromatic in the middle spring, and then becomes rougher and spicier as the weather warms; before it goes to flower, it becomes significantly drier. Gather the plant before flowering for the choicest leaves and flavor. However, it can be gathered and used anytime across the season: just use your nose and tastebuds to distinguish the flavor and quality.

How to Gather

Full stems of spearmint can be gathered, bundled, and dried for tea, or they can be used fresh in the kitchen. The fresh herb stores in the refrigerator for up to a week wrapped in a moist tea towel. But for maximum aromatics, process the plant immediately upon harvesting. Store in an airtight container to preserve the aromatics of the dried plant for later use.

How to Eat

Spearmint has a slightly different flavor than its cousin, peppermint. It's a less spicy and more cooling, relaxing herb. It works wonders as a refreshing flavor added to summer fruit salads or combined with savory flavors, like in chilled vegetable dishes such as fresh sugar snap pea salads, radish salads, or chilled locust blossom soup. Add it to a mixed berry compote and spoon over fresh local goat cheeses, yogurt, or ice cream.

Spearmint can also become a staple on your cocktail cart. Turn fresh spearmint into a simple syrup for mixed drinks, refreshing homemade sodas, iced teas, and spritzers. It mixes well with gins, vodkas, and dry champagnes.

Spearmint is also particularly useful for the home apothecary. Because of its relaxant nature, spearmint tea can soothe upset stomachs (and is gentle enough for wee ones) and soothe sore throats. The aromatics of the plant are also calming and can help ease away the stresses of the day before bedtime.

Future Harvests

Spearmint spreads through the soil with its underground runners, and gathering its stalks will do little to affect the plant's future growth and harvest.

spicebush

Lindera benzoin

EDIBLE berries, leaves, twigs

Spicebush is a native herb with a scent and flavor reminiscent of tropical allspice. Its berries, twigs, and leaves are all aromatic and can flavor baked goods and beverages, or be used in any recipe calling for allspice.

How to Identify

Spicebush is a small aromatic shrub, growing to heights of about 15 feet. It has dark-gray furrowed bark and alternate leaves that are smooth, oblong, and veined. It blooms in early spring and forms yellow-green flower clusters along the branches. The flowers bear red fruits (drupes) in late summer. The bark, leaves, and fruit are all aromatic.

Where and When to Gather

Spicebush prefers the hedgerows and partial sun of wooded areas. Gather the leaves and twigs anytime, and pick the berries in the late summer and fall.

Spicebush twigs, leaves, and berries can be made into a wonderful culinary spice similar in flavor to allspice.

How to Gather

Collect leaves, twigs, and berries by hand and lay them flat to dry. Be sure plant material is entirely dry—a dehydrator can be used to dry the berries—before storing it in an airtight container that will preserve the aromatics. When ready to use, the twigs can be powdered in a spice grinder; use a mortar and pestle to crush the berries and leaves.

How to Eat

Spicebush can be used in any recipe calling for allspice. The ground herb can be used to flavor pies, baked goods, cranberry sauce, or persimmon chutney. It offers a rich aromatic note to barbecue sauces and glazes, and works well with game meats like venison, duck, and wild pig. The flavor of spicebush pairs with full-bodied red wines like Cabernet, Zinfandel, Malbec, Syrah, and Petit Verdot. It can also be used to spice up a foraged chai blend of burdock, sarsaparilla, and sassafras.

Future Harvests

You can gather spicebush leaves, twigs, bark, and berries without significantly impacting future harvests. The shrub can be propagated by cuttings. It's a good plant to add to a permaculture landscape plan for areas of partial sun and shade.

spotted bee balm

Monarda punctata

spotted horsemint

`EDIBLE` leaves, flowers

Make no mistake: the delicate blossoms of spotted bee balm are not delicate at all. Rather these beauties carry a potent flavor—spicy and aromatic, similar to oregano—which you can gather for seasoning and teas.

How to Identify

Spotted bee balm is a perennial native, mint-family plant. Typically 6 to 8 inches tall but ranging up to 3 feet tall, it grows in stands connected by runners and prefers dry sandy soil in full sun. The stem is square, and leaves are opposite, slightly toothed, and slightly hairy. Its blooms are showy—creamy whitish green and with lilac spots—with large pink bracts below each blossom.

Spotted bee balm is an aromatic plant perfect for a culinary spice or tea. It is similar to oregano in flavor.

Where and When to Gather

The fresh spring leaves and stems of spotted bee balm can be gathered anytime and used in the kitchen fresh or dried. In mid- to late summer, the full stalk of the plant can be gathered (depending on the size of the stand—do not cut down full plants for their stems, as nothing will be left for the butterflies and honeybees).

How to Gather

Collect the stalks of spotted bee balm in warm, dry weather. The stalks can be bundled and dried for use as tea in the winter. Store all fully dry plant material in airtight containers to preserve the aromatics.

How to Eat

As a culinary spice, spotted bee balm can be used in pizzas, pasta sauces, chili, and other recipes that call for Italian seasoning combinations. Infuse this spicy herb in olive oil for a versatile aromatic oil that can be used for dipping bread or as a base for salad dressings.

Spotted bee balm can be infused into cold water for a refreshing summer iced tea. Its healing properties truly shine when brewed as a hot tea: its warming aromatics dispel the damp chill of a rainy day, can stimulate circulation in cold hands and feet, and soothe anyone suffering fever and chills. It also has excellent antimicrobial properties. Infuse its fresh flowers and leaves in honey to make a topical ointment for burns and fungal infections.

Future Harvests

For future harvests, cut only a portion of the plant to use for tea and leave some blossoms to go to seed. This is an easy-to-grow perennial that can be propagated by runners, cuttings, and transplants in the fall.

spring beauty

Claytonia species

`EDIBLE` flowers, leaves. stems

This tiny woodland wildflower pops up in early spring from beneath last season's leaf litter. The tender succulent plant has leaves with a fresh citrus flavor. It is a nice addition to a foraged spring salad or pretty garnish for a main dish.

How to Identify

Spring beauty is a small perennial plant that grows 3 to 6 inches in height. It has a tender, fleshy, succulent stem, with long, lance-shaped leaves that are green and smooth. Its flowers are white, with five pink-striped petals. The root system of spring beauty grows 2 to 3 inches beneath the soil and connects multiple plants.

Spring beauty's tiny flower is a perfect edible garnish for a salad or fish dish. Gather only a few flowers per stand to preserve future harvests.

Where and When to Gather

Spring beauty pushes up through the leaf litter of hardwood forests in early spring, alongside the trout lily, wild leek, mayapple, and morels. Look for it in areas of rich, well-drained soil, and in areas of partial sun. It grows across the Midwest; however, it may be more prolific in some areas than others, so harvest with this in mind.

How to Gather

To preserve future harvests of spring beauty, gather only a few leaves and flower stalks from each plant stand. While the root is edible, you would need a lot of them to make a serving worthwhile, and this could put a strain on existing stands. Cook immediately as the plant has little shelf life in the refrigerator.

How to Eat

Spring beauty lives up to its name in both appearance and in flavor. Nibble on a bit of the plant and you will find it slightly succulent and juicy, and somewhat fragrant with a sweet, lemony, green flavor. Because of its tiny size, spring beauty should be prepared with other foraged greens or vegetables. Its flower makes for a lovely garnish on spring salads of foraged greens. It can also withstand cooking and can be added to a frittata, a fritter of spring blossoms and greens (think locust blossom), or to top a chilled spring soup (again, think about using it with a chilled locust blossom soup). Use the pretty blossoms to garnish main dishes of fish (beautiful on the Easter or Passover table), lamb with mint sauce, or spring chicken.

Future Harvests

While the entire plant is edible, the only sustainable way to forage for spring beauty is to clip the aerial parts of the plant—the leaves, stems, and flowers—leaving the roots so the plant's stand may exist the following year.

spruce

Picea species

`EDIBLE` needles, shoots, tips

The bright citrus notes of new spruce needles give the chef a unique flavoring agent for use in cooking, baking, and cocktails.

How to Identify

Spruce is a tall conical evergreen, reaching heights of over 100 feet. The bark on the trunk is thin, dark gray-brown, and somewhat scaly. The branches grow in a whorled pattern with single, bluish, pointy needles growing at right angles to the branch on all sides. When the needles drop off, they leave a little peg behind that makes the twigs and branches rough to the touch.

Where and When to Gather

Spruce prefers moist soils and is common along stream banks and other water

The new tips and needles of the spruce can be used as a culinary spice, beer ingredient, and herbal remedy. Its flavor is not just for holiday time.

sources. It is common in the wild and in landscapes.

How to Gather
The new tips and shoots of the spruce in the early spring are choice to gather for eating. As the shoots develop into mature needles, they become more resinous, at which point they are still good to gather for herbal medicine–making.

How to Eat
Early spring spruce tips and young needles are notably bright, slightly sour, and citrusy in flavor, and they can be used in most recipes that call for lemony or rosemary flavors. The needles can be chopped and used as an herb to flavor salads, butters, and vinegars for dressings. Chopped spruce needles can also be added to potato salads, bean salads, and pasta salads with other fresh salad greens. Try them in rustic breads in place of rosemary. Water-soaked boughs and needles can be used to roast or steam white-fleshed fish.

For cocktails, spruce needles can be made into a simple syrup or infused into a honey that can flavor mixed drinks or martinis. Beer brewers interested in foraged ingredients can use the fresh spring spruce tips as a flavoring agent in the second fermentation cycle of brewing. A short fermentation will capture the desired aromatics and citrus high notes for a Belgian or wheat-styled ale without making the brew overly spruce-flavored.

Future Harvests
Harvest boughs, needles, and bark in a sustainable manner. As spruce is a common tree, gathering these plant parts in moderation will not impact future harvests.

sugar maple

Acer saccharum

EDIBLE sap

While most of the land is encrusted deep with snow in February, the sugar maple begins to awaken from a winter slumber and its sap begins to run, which means maple-syrup time has arrived.

How to Identify

Sugar maple is a beautiful deciduous tree, especially in late autumn when its green leaves turn vibrant hues of red, orange, and yellow. The densely branched sugar maple grows to 100 feet tall, with dark gray bark that becomes deeply furrowed as the sugar maple ages. The leaves are opposite and palmately lobed.

Where and When to Gather

While both birch and maple trees can be tapped for sap to be used in cooking, it's the sugar maple that produces that sweet, vanillin-flavored syrup we all know as real maple syrup. The sugar maple is found in mixed hardwood forests growing in rich, well-drained soil. The range in which this tree grows and sap is produced stretches

Sap collecting marks the beginning of the end of winter.

Sugar maples achieve dramatic shades of yellow, orange, and reds in the fall.

from the east across Canada into Vermont, as far west as Minnesota, and as far south as Louisiana. This limited production area makes real maple syrup a special treat and a specialty crop for tree farmers (and homesteading foragers) in the Midwest region.

How to Gather

Maple syrup harvest season begins when the weather stays above freezing for a few days with continued cold temperatures of 20 degrees F or so overnight. This usually is toward the middle to end of February.

To produce maple syrup in any quantity, identify maples of the right size. Tap only mature sugar maples at least 12 inches in diameter, placing the spike or tap about 4 to 5 feet off the ground. Hang a bucket off the tap, check it daily, and boil off the water to produce the desired maple "sugar" syrup.

How to Eat

Once you tap trees and boil your own maple syrup, you will never again wonder why the real deal in the grocery store is so pricey. It is liquid gold and should be

A Sweet Harvest: Making Maple Syrup

It takes on average about 60 gallons of sap from the sugar maple to produce one gallon of maple syrup. The length of the sap season varies from year to year according to the weather, anywhere from four to six weeks, but toward the end of the season, the quality and viscosity of the sap changes considerably and lessens in quality.

The forager should identify trees of the right size and age for tapping. Not only should the trees be of the proper size, but it's also helpful to have the trees close to where you will be processing the sap, as hauling, storing, and boiling down the sap is quite an operation.

Once the trees are tapped, collect the sap and deliver it to an established sugar shack—search for local farms and nature centers across the Midwest that have them on their properties. If there is no

Sap dripping to a collection bucket. It takes on average 60 gallons of sap to make one gallon of maple syrup.

sugar shack in your area, then you can build a temporary sap boiler outside to boil the sap down into syrup. Boiling off the water from the sap is a lengthy process that puts a lot of moisture into the air. Don't do it inside your home. Once the sap is boiled down into syrup, it can be poured into bottles and canned by water bath or stored into the refrigerator.

treated as such in the kitchen. From glazing Brussels sprouts to flavoring dressings, adding to coffee, and replacing cane sugar in baking, real maple syrup can be used for so much more than just pancakes. Try maple syrup in confections; a particular favorite is a French-style caramel. Make it with maple syrup (instead of cane sugar) with fresh local cream and butter to produce a decadent candy that has that deep vanilla flavor of maple syrup.

Real maple syrup is lower on the glycemic index than white sugar, honey, and agave syrup, and it contains minerals such as calcium, iron, and zinc. Because of this alone, consider replacing all chemically derived artificial sweeteners and white cane sugar with maple syrup.

Future Harvests

The biggest threat to the sugar maple and its ability to produce maple syrup is climate change and the increasing unpredictability of winter. This directly affects the sugaring season and the quality of syrup in general. For sustainable harvests, the forager should only tap mature trees so to not affect the growth of the younger ones.

sumac

Rhus typhina, R. glabra

`EDIBLE` drupes

There isn't anything more refreshing than a cool glass of sumac lemonade in the shade on a hot summer's day. Both species of red-fruited sumac offer tart and tangy berries (drupes) that can be used in beverages and desserts, and as a lemony spice.

How to Identify

Both of these common sumacs are deciduous perennial shrubs that grow up to 25 to 30 feet tall, but more commonly range from 3 to 10 feet tall. They have smooth gray bark, with alternate compound leaves of up to 30 toothed, lance-shaped leaflets that also smell citrusy. The yellowish-white flowers bloom in upright, Christmas-tree shaped clusters that turn into deep red drupes in late summer. These clusters remain red through the winter and are attached to the tops of the leafless stems, making it easy to identify the plant in the winter.

The species are easily distinguished: the drupes of the staghorn sumac (*Rhus typhina*) are fuzzy, as they are covered with velvet hairs. The drupes of the smooth sumac (*Rhus glabra*) have a wrinkled skin coating but are hairless. The stem below the fruit cluster of the staghorn sumac is velvety, with fine hairs on a tan-colored stem, which resembles the velveted antlers of a stag (male deer), hence the name.

Where and When to Gather

Both sumacs are common native shrubs and can be easily spotted growing in clonal stands in partial sun along road banks, hedgerows, bordering fields, and woodlands. The flower clusters ripen into deep red fruit clusters toward the end of July and into early September.

How to Gather

Taste a pinch of the drupes. If the pinch tastes sour, with a pleasant aftertaste, collect these drupes. If, on the other hand, the taste is barely sour, move on to another patch. When you find the perfect plant, use hand pruners to gather into a bucket the clusters that are most bright in color and most uniformly red.

Once you get home, you won't want to wash the berries as that will wash out the aromatics and flavor, so pick as cleanly as you can and choose only those clusters that are free of significant dust. Use the harvest immediately or put them in the refrigerator for use within the week. Alternately, you can dry the clusters in a dehydrator, then

Staghorn sumac drupes are citrusy in flavor and make a delicious pink lemonade perfect for summertime sipping and garden parties.

shake off the drupes (removing any other debris), and then store them in the freezer for up to several years.

How to Eat

The tangy lemon flavor of the sumac's red drupes make for a versatile and delicious culinary herb. Only a few tablespoons of the drupes infused in several cups of water are enough to make a pink lemonade-like drink. Strain, sweeten with honey or maple syrup, and voila! Kids will delight that you can make lemonade without lemons.

If you are serving a group, put 4 cups of drupes into a gallon pitcher and add 3 quarts of cold water. Stir with a wooden spoon for a few minutes, and smash drupes a bit to release more of the flavor and pink coloring. Strain this through a dishtowel into another container. Sweeten to taste, and add ice before drinking.

Increase the ratio of drupes to water and simmer to create a concentrate that can be converted into a lemon-flavored simple syrup for refreshing sodas, summer shandies (think pairing it with a GoldenRod

Belgian Ale), and mixed drinks. The simple syrup can also be used in panna cottas, ice cream, meringue, and to top fresh yogurt. To decorate desserts, use the drupes as a plate garnish (but note, there are seeds inside, so use the berries to dress the plate instead of garnishing the food directly).

The drupes can also be used in the Middle Eastern za'atar paste with foraged bee balm, delicious over yellow dock crackers, or use them to top local feta cheese for a savory snack. Make a simple rub for chicken or fish by rubbing the drupes of smooth sumac against the mesh of a kitchen strainer set on top of a bowl.

Future Harvests

Sumacs are common shrubs. You can gather the ripe, red clusters without worry of impacting future harvests.

sunchoke

Helianthus tuberosus

Jerusalem artichoke

`EDIBLE` tubers

Sunchokes are a good source of carbohydrates. The tubers have a crunchy texture and nutty flavor similar to those of the groundnut.

How to Identify

Sunchoke is a perennial wildflower that grows in clusters that are 4 to 10 feet tall. Its leaves are dry, rough, and hairy, with a pointed oval shape. Lower to the ground, the leaves are arranged oppositely along the stem, then alternately toward the flower. The flower blooms from August into September and is bright yellow with 10 to 20 petals arranged in rays, like the sunflower. The flower, however, has a yellow center as opposed to the brown center of many sunflowers.

The tubers can range in size from spindly as a finger or, if gathered in rich, well-drained, and composted soil, knobby and substantial (especially if they are wild tubers escaped from long abandoned

Sunchoke flowers bloom in late summer and into early fall in large, tall stands.

These sunchoke tubers, though found growing wild, escaped from cultivation and are larger than the typical wild sunchoke.

gardens), about the size of cultivated ginger and ranging in lengths from 2 to 6 inches.

Where and When to Gather

Look for sunchoke in wet fields, ditches, and along stream beds. It is frequently found alongside cow parsnip and groundnut. Look for its tall yellow flowers. Soon after the plant begins to die back, the tubers can be harvested. Cultivated sunchoke sometimes escapes the farm and garden, so abandoned fields with moist, well-drained soil can often be good locations to find it.

How to Gather

Bring a small shovel to turn the soil and dig the tubers. These can be cleaned and then kept in cold storage, as well as chopped, blanched, and frozen for later use.

How to Eat

Uncooked sunchokes can have a strong gaseous effect on the stomach, and for some folks, even cooked sunchokes can cause stomach gas. Parboiling and fermenting the tuber can help digestibility significantly. Sunchokes can be prepared similarly to the cultivated Jerusalem artichoke. They also make an excellent mellow-flavored, fermented pickle similar to Korean kimchee.

Like the groundnut, sunchoke is an excellent filler in recipes and has a neutral enough flavor to work well with spices ranging from curry and Latin flavors to French and Asian directions. Roast the tubers with carrots and beets, or sauté them with a rich garlic and sage butter. The tubers can be roasted and creamed into a rich soup as well as thrown into a stir-fry with other foraged flavors like wild ginger.

Future Harvests

You can help guarantee future harvests by digging and turning the soil where tubers are found so they can spread and establish a new colony via new rhizomes.

sweet clover

Melilotus alba, M. officinalis

EDIBLE flowers, seed, stalk

Sweet clover's heady notes of vanilla and honey waft through the air in summer. You can capture its fragrant summer essence for baking, beverages, and for use in the herbal apothecary.

How to Identify

Sweet clover is a tall, biennial, herbaceous plant that grows up to 6 feet tall. Its dull green stalk is tall and erect, branched, and smooth. The trifoliate, oblong leaves are alternate along the stem, and the small flower clusters are white or yellow. The entire plant smells distinctly of mowed grass and vanilla.

Where and When to Gather

Sweet clover is a common cover crop used to fix nitrogen in the soil, but it is also found in other areas of poor soil quality, such as in ditches and disturbed areas. It grows abundantly and escapes from cultivation enough to qualify it in some areas as a noxious weed. Sweet clover blooms in late June through early August and goes to seed shortly thereafter.

Sweet clover (*Melilotus alba*) has a strong scent of vanilla that fills the air in summertime.

Yellow sweet clover (*Melilotus officinalis*) can be used similarly. Just use your nose to gauge the strength of the vanilla scent.

How to Gather

Sweet clover should be gathered while it is in full bloom on a dry, sunny day. The blossoms should be processed immediately or dried for later use. The plant's stalk can be cut down entirely and then hung to dry in a cool, dry place with good ventilation so it does not mold. The seeds of the dried plant can be gathered and collected for a culinary spice.

How to Eat

The plant's heady vanilla aroma is of most use to you in the kitchen. Its dried seeds can be crushed and used to add vanilla scent to baking projects or herbal beverages like a foraged chai.

The unwilted blossoms of sweet clover can be transformed into a sweet-smelling hydrosol (or floral water) that is similar to rosewater but with strong vanilla notes. Dry blossoms can also be used to make a hydrosol, as long as they are mold free. The hydrosol can be used in a variety of cooking projects including flavoring shortbreads, biscotti, and cakes, and for poaching fruits. The hydrosol can be sweetened and converted into a simple syrup used to flavor ice cream or sweeten plain yogurt, sorbet, panna cotta, and meringue.

The sweet clover hydrosol also has a use in the herbal apothecary, as its uplifting scent is a remedy to dispel melancholy. The spray can be misted on the skin and face as a cooling facial mist. Dried bundles of sweet clover can be added to your home's decor as attractive dried flower arrangements, which will also give off sweet clover's summer aroma well into the winter.

Future Harvests

Sweet clover is a beneficial plant that improves poor-quality soil, but because it is a voracious spreader, it is qualified as a noxious weed by many native plant folk. Gathering the plant by the armful will do little to impact future harvests or the plant's sustainability.

Caution

Because of its chemical compounds that include the presence of coumadin, those on pharmaceutical blood thinners should avoid working with and consuming sweet clover.

sweet pea

Lathyrus latifolius

EDIBLE peapods, peas, shoots

Sweet pea sprawls along rocky, sandy soils and is easy to recognize with its bright magenta flowers that give way to delicious, petite peapods that you can enjoy in salads, soups, and stir-fries.

How to Identify

Sweet pea is a waxy green sprawling vine that climbs over nearby vegetation and can spread up to 6–8 feet. Tall, erect, and angular flower stalks shoot up in late spring that produce beautiful magenta, pea-like flowers that bloom into late summer. The flowers bear small pea pods about

Sweet pea has broad wings on the stem and petioles. The leaf has two leaflets and one tendril on the end.

The wild sweet pea (*Lathyrus latifolius*) is similar to the cultivated sweet pea. Its pods, shoots, and peas are delicious in salads, stir-fries, and soups.

A relative of sweet pea, the edible beach pea (*Lathyrus japonicus*) is common to the Great Lakes, shown here in flower on the northern Lake Michigan shoreline in midsummer. The pods are edible, though sweet pea is better in flavor and texture.

2 inches in length that have small tiny edible peas inside. The leaf has only two leaflets and one tendril on the end, and there are broad wings on the stem and petioles.

Where and When to Gather

Sweet pea thrives in sandy or rocky soils. Its spring shoots can be used as greens in soups or stir-fries. The fresh pods appear as early as late June and continue to be abundant into August.

How to Gather

Gather tender, young shoots in mid- to late spring. Fresh, ripe peapods will be firm to the touch. They can be cleaned and prepared fresh. For later use, blanch them whole or shelled, then freeze them. The dry, brown pods gathered in late summer and fall can be shelled and their contents used as dry peas.

How to Eat

Use the pea shoots raw in salads, sautéed, or cooked in soups. The fresh sweet pea is similar in taste to the cultivated snow pea, but is firmer in texture. To cook the pods, blanch them in salted water and then add to a stir-fry, puree them into soup, or just eat them with garlic and butter.

The peas, while petite, can be shelled and used in pasta dishes, salads, or soups. The pods and shelled peas can be blanched and frozen and used similarly later in the season. Use the dry peas for a delicious foraged pea soup or grind them into flour for use in a gluten-free flour mixture.

Future Harvests

Sweet pea is a fast-growing, abundant wild weed, and your harvest will do little to threaten the plant's sustainability.

thimbleberry

Rubus parviflorus

EDIBLE berries

Thimbleberry's soft, red, tart fruit makes a perfect snack along the trail, and if any berries make it back to the ranch, they can be converted into the coveted thimbleberry jam, fruit leather, and pie.

How to Identify

The thimbleberry bush has glandular hairs instead of thorns and grows to 6 feet tall. Its simple, maple-like leaves have palmate venation, with five lobes, and are sharply toothed. The leaves alternate along the cane. Thimbleberry has white flowers in late spring that develop into soft red fruit that is up to ¾ inch across in late summer. The fruit grows in clusters and is seedy, tart, and soft; it resembles a wide raspberry with smaller, drier-looking carpels.

Flowers of the thimbleberry in early summer.

Thimbleberry is a delicious, quintessential fruit of the northern Midwest found in many a homemade jam or pie.

Where and When to Gather

Thimbleberry likes to grow along the trail, in part sun, at the edges of woods and open fields. Its fruits ripen in late July into early August.

How to Gather

The fruits are soft and do not travel well. Gather them into shallow baskets so as to not crush them. Process immediately in the kitchen or freeze for later use.

How to Eat

Like its cousins the raspberry and black-berry, thimbleberry makes for delicious crumbles, pies, and muffins. The fruits also make a delicious jam and fruit leather, but because the fruit is especially seedy, run it through a food mill or strainer first. For beverages, you can ferment the thimble-berry into wine or macerate crushed thim-bleberries with raw apple cider vinegar to create a refreshing and nutritious vin-egar shrub. A simple thimbleberry syrup can flavor mixed drinks, champagnes, and refreshing homemade sodas.

Future Harvests

Thimbleberry propagates easily in open wooded areas and along disturbed edges of woods, and it transplants well. The plants are a good addition to a permaculture land-scape plan. Harvesting the fruits will have little impact on future harvests.

trout lily

Erythronium americanum

`EDIBLE` leaves

Trout lily is a petite, woodland ephemeral that blankets the forest floor in early spring across the Midwest. The leaves of this plant are succulent, tangy, and juicy. They taste slightly of lemon—a perfect addition to the foraged greens of a spring salad.

How to Identify

The succulent, waxy basal leaves grow from small bulbs. They are lance-shaped, mottled with a purple-brownish patterning, and grow to be 2 to 4 inches in length. Each plant has a single or clustered yellow flower on a leafless stalk.

Where and When to Gather

Trout lily pushes up from the leaf litter on the hardwood forest floor in early spring surrounded by mayapple, wild leek, spring beauty, and morels.

Tender trout lily in bloom in the early spring woods. Gather only a few leaves from each stand to preserve future harvests.

The tender, succulent leaves of trout lily.

How to Gather

To sustainably gather this spring ephemeral, gather no more than one leaf per plant, and while the bulb or corm is edible, it should remain in the ground so as not to diminish the plant's distribution. The leaves can be gently washed if needed and then stored in the refrigerator in a paper bag for one to two days.

How to Eat

The leaves have a juicy, tart, lemon flavor and slightly crunchy texture. This makes for a nice addition to a foraged green salad, helping temper the bitters of any other wild spring greens like dock, dandelion, or garlic mustard. Trout lily leaves can also be chopped and added to a fresh Vietnamese spring roll in place of bean sprouts, or added to a hot bowl of pho. The leaves can also be added at the end of a stir-fry or tossed into a pad Thai dish before serving.

Future Harvests

Trout lily is a spring wildflower and not widely distributed in all areas. Gather only a leaf from each plant (leave the plant and bulb in place) to help ensure the viability of the plant for future enjoyment.

tulip tree

Liriodendron tulipifera

EDIBLE branches, flowers

The tulip tree stands tall, with showy, tulip-like flowers that you can use in early summer, along with new twigs and branches, as a culinary herb. They have a delicate, clove-like spice flavor that works nicely in a bitters blend or as a baking flavoring agent and herbal remedy.

Tulip tree blossoms are both beautiful and spicy. They are useful as an herbal medicine.

How to Identify

Tulip tree is tall and erect, growing to heights well over 100 feet with dark gray, furrowed bark. Its leaves are smooth, 3 to 5 inches wide, alternate, palmate, and lobed. The flowers are remarkable and resemble a tulip or a tea cup: these are bright, showy, single blooms that decorate the tall tree with green, yellow, and orange colors. The fruit is a 3-inch brown cone that develops in late fall and is a good marker for off-season identification.

Where, and When to Gather

Tulip tree grows across the middle and southeastern part of the Midwest and prefers milder, temperate growing locations. Its new branches and flowers can be gathered in late June into early July.

Sometimes a big summer thunderstorm or bout of high winds will bring down a significant number of brittle branches that have both the new tips of branches and flowers. These are easiest to gather, particularly as the rest of the small branches and blooms are completely out of reach. Cut the new tips and branches into small pieces to dry, or process them into simple syrup and plant extracts. Fallen green wood can also be used for grilling.

How to Eat

The flowers and tips of tulip tree branches have a warming spice flavor and make a useful culinary herb. The blooms are slightly resinous and can be dried, but work best when made into a simple syrup with the new branch tips. When you make

Tulip tree bark and leaves.

Tulip trees are fast-growing, tall, and erect with brittle wood. The branches begin very high up on the tree, and it is a light wood with many uses, including dugout canoes.

plant extract (see page 46) that is useful as a flavoring agent in baking and cocktail making. A high-proof alcohol is recommended to extract the resins of the plant, but a locally made rum also works delightfully well as the spiciness of the rum complements the spices of the plant.

The aromatic spicy notes in the plant extract can be used as a layer in a cocktail bitters blend, offering a warming flavor and carminative effect that can soothe a stomach upset from overindulgence. Traditionally, herbalists use the tulip tree to help stimulate digestion. A tulip tree bitters blend can be made with other plants like burdock, yellow dock, coffee (not local, I know), basil, and orange peel. Sweeten with a bit of maple syrup and use liberally in cocktail drinks or add to a homemade soda.

The green planks of the tree, harvested in the spring and soaked in water, can be used to impart the tulip tree flavor on the grill for meats, fish, and vegetables.

Future Harvests

The tulip tree is a fast-growing hardwood, and gathering its fallen branches and flowers after a storm will do little to impact the tree's future harvests. The tree can be easily propagated by saplings.

the infusion for the simple syrup, keep it covered to preserve the delicate and fleeting aromatic oils of the plant. Tulip tree simple syrup works well in recipes that use maple syrup instead of cane sugar, creating a richer flavor profile that enhances the tree's delicate spice.

The flowers and tips of the branches can also be extracted into alcohol to make a

violet

Viola species

EDIBLE flowers, leaves

Violet leaves have a mild, bright, slightly lemon flavor and are an easily foraged gateway food to get friends and family interested in "eating the weeds." Its flowers are pretty and delicious, too.

How to Identify

Violet is a small herbaceous perennial that has soft, heart-shaped leaves arranged in a basal rosette. The flowers, which extend on short stems from the axils of the leaf, are five-petaled and bilaterally symmetrical. They range in color from white to white-blue to purple and often hybridize.

Where and When to Gather

Violets grow abundantly in the dappled shade of fields and disturbed places, or in lawns of untreated grasses. The plant begins to unfurl in early April and continues to grow and bloom through May. It begins to die back in summer and then reappears with another set of leaves to

Violet leaves are one of my favorite early spring greens, delicious and tender in a spring salad.

Violet flowers are edible in salads and confections and are delightful candied. Harvest before spring rains damage the delicate blossoms.

gather later in the fall when the rains return.

How to Gather

Leaves can be picked by hand by the basketful. Choose leaves that are relatively clean and dirt free. They will store one to two days in the refrigerator in a moist towel; wash when ready to use. The flowers should be picked on a dry day as excess rain and moisture can damage the fragile blooms. The blooms can be dried on a screen for later use, but be forewarned—what looks like a large gathering of blossoms will dry down to about one-tenth the size. But they are so pretty, it's worth the effort.

How to Eat

Violet leaves are high in vitamin C and are delicious as a raw vegetable, with a bright and slightly lemon flavor. Add them to a wild foraged salad or combine with chickweed to make a foraged green smoothie blend. Violet flowers are also a forager's spring delight. The flowers are lovely as a garnish on salads (children will delight in picking them for their dinner plate). An infusion of the flowers can be transformed into a deep purple tea, which can help soothe a sore throat and clear lymphatic congestion from a spring cold.

The infusion can also be made into a simple syrup for cocktails, as well as the base for a violet flower jelly. The jelly will

Dry the violet blossoms for a nice herbal tisane.

become a vibrant fuchsia when lemon juice is added—another kid-friendly foraging project. Spoon the jelly over fresh spring goat cheese and garnish with a few candied violet flowers. Simple and perfect.

Future Harvests

Violet is a common spring plant and gathering its leaves and flowers will not impact future harvests. Clumps of violets can easily be transplanted if you want to help grow the stand of violets for future gathering.

watercress

Nasturtium officinale

EDIBLE stems and leaves

Watercress is popular in specialty groceries and restaurants, but you can seek out its robust, peppery flavor (for free) each spring.

How to Identify

Watercress is a perennial dark green herbaceous plant that grows up to 12 inches in height. Its slightly waxy compound leaves are arranged in a basal rosette. The stems are hollow, and the flowers appear in tiny, dense, white flower heads. Small white rootlets grow from the joints of stems, which float in the water.

Where and When to Gather

Watercress is an aquatic or semi-aquatic plant, so you can find it in moving streams and along the edges of marshes. The plant is perfect for harvesting in early spring through early summer. Make sure you collect where there is no potential runoff from nearby farms, golf courses, or industry.

Watercress can be found in abundance in clear running streams.

How to Gather

Watercress stems and leaves can be gathered by the bunch. It can be stored in damp towels in the refrigerator for a few days before it wilts.

How to Eat

The plant is slightly bitter, with a peppery bite, a good addition to a deli-style sandwich or pita wrap. Or use watercress to garnish small radish and butter sandwiches, or a rich grilled goat cheese sandwich on sourdough.

In salads, watercress blends unusually well with fruits like avocado, watermelon, orange, and tangerine. Add fresh green onion and cilantro to this combo for a spunky fruit salsa for fish or pork. Watercress is durable enough to cook and can be stir-fried with other early spring greens or tossed into an egg frittata, quiche, or spring greens tart topped with goat cheese. Watercress can also be incorporated into pasta dishes like orzo or gnocchi and topped with a buttery sauce of wild morel mushrooms.

As for soups, watercress greens can be added to a steaming hot bowl of pho. And in the name of simplicity, the cooked puree of watercress and spring potatoes makes a perfectly delicious soup. Garnish with spring onions and wild garlic.

Future Harvests

Watercress grows abundantly and can be easily cultivated. It is a perennial, so that harvesting the green tops will not significantly affect future harvests. More concern, however, should be given to ensure clean watersheds and waterways, which will allow wild watercress to thrive alongside other wetland and marsh plants.

white clover

Trifolium repens

`EDIBLE` blossoms

Growing in abundance in open fields, gardens, and even between the sidewalk cracks, white clover is a bright-flavored, nutritious weed that you can gather with abandon to add to teas and soups.

White clover is as plentiful as its red cousin and can be used similarly.

How to Identify

White clover is a low-growing plant that can cover the ground, though it stands as tall as 2 feet in some areas. The plant has three soft leaflets per leaf, and the leaves are arranged alternately along the stem. The stem is hairless. Clover begins to blossom in June, featuring a showy white bloom head comprised of many small, nectar-filled, tubular florets.

Where and When to Gather

White clover grows abundantly in sunny, open spaces and can tolerate both moist and dry soil. It begins to bloom around the solstice and remains in bloom throughout the summer. White clover can easily take up minerals, including heavy metals like lead, so harvest clover in areas free of soil contamination.

How to Gather

Gather the blossoms by hand on a dry, sunny day. Choose only the flowers that are vibrant and free of brown withering. Do not gather blossoms that are damp or moist as they will wilt or could mold while drying. Harvest only in areas that are free from pesticides, nitrate pollution, and heavy metal contamination. The blossoms can be prepared fresh or dried on screens for later use.

How to Eat

White clover blossoms are mineral-rich and contain calcium, potassium, and magnesium, to name a few. The blossoms have a green taste and can be eaten fresh, but they are a bit dry to incorporate into a salad. They do work well in a greens fritter, egg dish, or soups. The blossoms can also be steamed and have a flavor similar to the sweet pea. They make a nice accompanying garnish or side dish for a light white fish.

In addition to eating the blossoms, to fully enjoy white clover's mineral density, you can extract fresh or dry plant material in a long infusion of hot water or boil for 20 minutes to release the minerals. White clover mixes well in this sort of infusion with nettle, oat straw, horsetail, or raspberry to make a nutrient-dense beverage that can be enjoyed as an iced tea or at room temperature, or added to smoothies, soups, or stews. It can also be used to soak beans, lentils, or rice, or to cook pasta to infuse the carbohydrates with additional nutrition.

Future Harvests

White clover is an abundant edible wild plant. A perennial, it comes back easily after gathering or even mowing. Gathering the blossoms and green tops will not affect future harvests.

Caution

There has been some debate over white clover's possible effects on hormone balance, but traditional use suggests it is safe for general consumption as food.

white lettuce

Nabalus albus

EDIBLE leaves

White lettuce is another bitter wild green that is not as well known to many foragers, but is as versatile as dandelion, dock, or wild lettuce.

White lettuce growing in a small stand in the woods.

How to Identify

White lettuce is a small, unassuming biennial plant with lone basal leaves that are smooth and flat, and which grow relatively parallel to the ground on a leaf stem 6 to 8 inches in height. The leaf shape is variable: some are arrow-shaped, some are lobed, some grow to be only 4 inches across, and some up to 12 inches in length. The younger leaves are slightly waxy and tender, growing more bitter and rough as the plant gets ready to send up its flower stalk in late summer. The flower stalk grows to 6 feet or more, and it is branched with very showy pink and white composite flower heads that bloom in August.

Where and When to Gather

White lettuce is found in areas of dappled sun, in the woods and along trails. The basal leaves are unassuming and begin to push out in springtime as the mayapple dies back. The plant's leaves are choice in the early spring, before the plant goes to flower. Once the stalk emerges, the leaves become significantly more bitter.

How to Gather

White lettuce grows singly or in stands depending on the distribution of the plant. Gather the leaves by hand. The leaves should be harvested sparingly to not damage the plant's ability to photosynthesize. Prepare upon harvesting.

How to Eat

The flavor and texture of white lettuce are more or less similar to that of dandelion or tender wild lettuce. Use as salad greens in a foraged salad with violets, trout lily, and watercress, or top sandwiches with a handful of the greens. To temper the bitterness, massage the greens with a lemon juice and mustard vinaigrette.

Future Harvests

While not an endangered plant, white lettuce can be sparingly distributed in the forests and at the edges of the woods. To harvest the plant sustainably, gather only a few leaves from each plant so it can continue to grow and propagate.

white pine

Pinus strobus

EDIBLE boughs, needles

There is no finer way to bring the aroma of the forest into the kitchen and onto the plate than by foraging pine boughs and needles. Pine's bright citrus notes offer the chef a unique flavoring agent for cooking, cocktails, and herbal remedies.

The needles of white pine are aromatic and rich in vitamin C.

How to Identify

White pine is a tall conifer, reaching heights of over 120 feet. Its bark is a
smooth greenish gray, with soft, long, and
flexible needles that cluster in groups of
five. A mnemonic device to remember with
identification: there is one needle in each
cluster for each of the letters in the word
"white."

Where and When to Gather

Look for pines in the sandy soils of beaches
and old farmsteads. It likes acidic soil and
grows in large stands. Needles can be collected anytime, but are most tender and
aromatic in the springtime.

How to Gather

Pine needles pine can be easily gathered
by hand. Collect boughs that fall from the
trees after a strong windstorm.

How to Eat

Bringing pine into the kitchen is like bringing the aroma of the forest to the table. The
needles are notably bright, slightly sour,
and citrusy in flavor, and they can be used
in most recipes that call for lemon.

Chop the needles and use them as an
herb to flavor salads, butters, and vinegars
for dressings. They can also be added to
potato salads, bean salads, and pasta salads with other fresh salad greens. Use them
to flavor rustic breads in place of rosemary.
Water-soaked boughs and needles can be
used to roast or steam white-fleshed fish.
Pine-infused honey can be drizzled over ice
cream (or can flavor ice cream) or can be
served with Stilton or cheddar cheese. It is
a delicious way to savor the magical forest
flavor.

For cocktails, pine needles can be made
into a simple syrup or infused honey that
can flavor mixed drinks or martinis. Beer
brewers interested in using foraged ingredients can use the fresh pine tips as a flavoring agent in the second fermentation
cycle of brewing. A short fermentation will
capture the desired aromatics and citrus
high notes for a Belgian or wheat-styled
ale without making the brew overly pine
flavored.

As an herbal remedy, pine needles can
be made into a tea. Add boiling water to a
pot of needles, cover, and let steep for 3 to
5 minutes. Sweeten with honey, sip, and
inhale the aromatics.

Future Harvests

Harvest boughs and needles in a sustainable manner by gathering them from fallen
branches after a windy storm. Pine can be
propagated in acidic soils with seedlings,
and advocacy for habitat loss will also help
grow the distribution of the white pine
across the Midwest.

wild carrot

Daucus carota
Queen Anne's lace

`EDIBLE` leaves, roots, seeds

Wild carrot decorates the summer grasslands alongside the wild
and edible chicories. It brings the scent of carrot to dishes through
its roots, leaves, and seeds.

How to Identify

A petite biennial plant, wild carrot is a
wispy member of the family Apiaceae,
which includes the poisonous look-alike
poison hemlock—*Conium maculatum*
(shown on page 47). However, there are
several chief identifiers of the wild carrot.
The first-year leaves of the wild carrot are
feathery, and true leaves are pinnately
divided and deeply cut into narrow segments. There will be small vertical hairs
on the leaf stems. The second-year plant

The flower of wild carrot is easily identified by the bract beneath the umbel, its hairy stem, and carroty smell.
These are three significant indicators to distinguish wild carrot from poison hemlock.

The wild carrot root is white and more spindly than that of a cultivated carrot.

sends up a thin but stately and hairy stem of up to 4 feet in height. The hairy stem is green and devoid of the purple markings that might be prevalent on poison hemlock.

Wild carrot blooms in late July and into August with an umbel made up of flat and wide white, small, and terminal flowers. Take care to notice the branched bracts that fringe the bottom of the umbel of the wild carrot (another chief identifier). Sometimes (but not always) there is a dark purple flower in the center of the umbel. The umbel begins to close and seeds begin to develop in early fall.

The entire plant has a noticeable smell of carrot. In the absence of that smell, you may be handling another plant. Do not taste it. Take care in handling plants in the Apiaceae family: the toxins of poison hemlock and poison water hemlock can be absorbed through the skin, so only handle them with gloves.

Where and When to Gather

Wild carrot is widespread across the Midwest and is prolific in disturbed areas, along roads, and in open grassy fields. The seeds will begin to develop and ripen in late summer.

Another identifier of wild carrot is the bract below the flower head.

How to Gather

If harvesting in poor quality soil that is really dry and rocky, or if growing conditions have been especially dry, take along a digging fork so as to not break off the root in the ground. To harvest the root, properly identify a first-year plant as its root will be less woody and spindly. The feathery tops can be harvested for greens, but wash these carefully as sand can be easily caught up in the textured leaves.

Gather the umbels in the morning in sunny weather, taking care that they are free of bugs (they are a favorite haven for daddy long-legged spiders) and debris.

Because of the fragile nature of the blossoms, try to harvest clean so they don't have to be washed.

Gather the seeds in late summer when the "nest" of seeds has browned and they are dry, taking care to gather before the fall rains arrive, as excess moisture will rob the seeds of their aromatic carrot flavor.

How to Eat

The roots of wild carrot are significantly smaller than those of the cultivated carrot, but have a nuttier flavor similar to the parsnip. Eating the fresh roots raw is a bit difficult as they are tough. Boil and

The seed heads fold upward, making a bird's nest shape when the seeds are dry and ready for harvesting. The crushed and dried seeds of wild carrot can be used as a culinary spice in soups and stews.

mash the young roots, but you will need more than just a handful to make a substantial meal. You can combine the boiled wild carrot root with the prepared root of Solomon's seal for a complex and flavorful starch dish. Chop and toss fresh young wild carrot leaves into a salad of wild greens to give it the herbed flavor of carrot.

Enjoy the umbels in a wild greens fritter, using other foraged finds like purslane and even chicories for density and substance. The seeds can be used to flavor any variety of dishes, including soups and stews, with an aromatic carrot flavor. Crush them first in a mortar and pestle instead of adding whole, as the seed is slightly hairy and can pose an issue to those sensitive to texture.

Future Harvests

Wild carrot grows in abundance in wild grassy areas and disturbed waste places. In some areas it is deemed invasive, so harvesting this wildflower will pose little threat to the plant's future sustainability.

wild ginger
Asarum canadense
EDIBLE rhizome

The wild ginger that carpets the early spring woods isn't a relative of the culinary ginger, *Zingiber officinale*, and it isn't traditionally used as a kitchen spice. However, the rhizome of wild ginger has a unique acrid and spicy aromatic flavor can be integrated into earthy culinary recipes that will tolerate its strong taste.

How to Identify

Wild ginger is a low-growing perennial woodland wildflower, with two heart-shaped basal leaves emerging from the ground in early spring. The dark green veined leaves grow to be not much larger than 4 to 6 inches in height, and its purple flower blooms close to the ground in later

The acrid flavor of the wild ginger rhizome makes for a strong culinary spice.

spring. The edible part of the plant, the rhizome, runs between plants. It is small, creamy white, relatively spindly, and aromatic with an acrid smell of spicy ginger.

Where and When to Gather

Wild ginger grows abundantly in rich, well-drained soil. It tolerates shade. Frequently, it is found blanketing the ground in woodland areas. The wild ginger root is notably more spindly than cultivated ginger root. Gathering the root en masse will stress the plant population, so gather with care and never dig up the entire plant, making sure to leave pieces of root so the plant can remain established for future harvests. The root (or stolon or rhizome) of wild ginger can be gathered in spring and fall. Clean and chop the root, then dry it in a dehydrator. Store in an airtight container to preserve the aromatics.

How to Eat

The aroma of wild ginger is reminiscent of cultivated ginger found at the grocery store, but it's more acrid, nearly peppery. To best understand its flavor, take a nibble. Its dynamic flavor can be used in some recipes that call for the more mild cultivated ginger in cooking or as a flavoring agent in beverages and for tea.

The root can be made into a delicious simple syrup for cocktails, sodas, or desserts. To make a warm spiced milk, boil the root in milk and then strain and sweeten the preparation with honey and cinnamon: it soothes an upset stomach and relieves bloating caused by overindulgence. The root can also be dried, roasted, and added in small quantities to a foraged chai blend to add an earthy, spicy layer.

Future Harvests

Gather wild ginger root between the bud shoots to allow for the plant to regenerate, and make sure to leave pieces of root so the plant can remain established for future harvests.

wild grape

Vitis riparia

EDIBLE flowers, fruit, leaves

Wild grape doesn't hide: it creeps across open lands, climbing on fences and over abandoned property in the summer sun. In spring, enjoy its greens; in summer, its fruit. And it's perfect for preserving in fall.

Wild grapes are a delicious fall fruit for juice and jellies.

Wild grape leaves can be pickled and used in stuffed grape leaf rolls, or dolmas.

How to Identify

Wild grape is a deciduous perennial that is easily identifiable by its climbing, woody vine. It has dark, shaggy, hairless (unlike poison ivy) bark with yellow-green coiling tendrils that affix the vine to fences, buildings, and anything else it can cling to. The dark green grape leaves unfurl in early spring and grow alternately along the vine to be 3 to 5 inches in diameter, deeply lobed and toothed. The underside of the leaf is silvery green and deeply veined. The leaves become thicker and bug-damaged over the growing season.

Wild grape flowers are tiny and greenish white. They grow in clusters that will then ripen into clusters of the dark purple grapes. Wild grapes are significantly smaller than the cultivated grape and only grow to 1/2 to 1 inch in diameter, each with two to six seeds inside.

Where and When to Gather

Wild grape grows abundantly in open spaces, along fences at parks, and along buildings. It climbs up trees and spreads over abandoned lots. Collect the tender leaves and flowers in the spring for salads. The wild grape is ready in the fall and is sweeter and less tart after a hard fall frost.

How to Gather

When you collect the leaves and flowers in spring, be sure to leave enough flowers for fall's fruits. The wild grapes of fall can be gathered in bunches.

How to Eat

In early spring, tender young grape leaves can be added to a salad, and the flowers are a nice aromatic to add as an edible garnish. When the leaves grow a bit larger in summer, they can be pickled and used for dolmas, or stuffed grape leaves.

In the fall, wild grapes are a fine fruit to enjoy on the trail. They can be processed similar to Concord grapes. The grapes can be smashed and processed into juice for drinking or fermenting, or for wild grape jelly or fruit leather. Remove the seeds first with a food mill.

Future Harvests

Wild grape grows with wild abandon, and you can gather buckets of the fruit and leaves without impacting future harvests.

wild leek

Allium tricoccum

ramps

`EDIBLE` bulb, leaves

An early spring ephemeral, the wild leek—or ramps—is an aromatic, delicious wild onion. The bulb sweetens when roasted, pickles well for martinis, and has tops that are delicious as garnish or incorporated into a spring salad. But harvest with care: recent popularity has threatened it.

How to Identify

Wild leek is an early spring bulb that is markedly oniony in both flavor and scent. It could easily be confused with false hellebore and lily of the valley, both of which are poisonous and neither of which smells or tastes like onion. If in doubt, scratch and sniff.

Wild leeks are an early spring delicacy. Clip the top greens only for sustainable harvesting.

It takes about 18 months for a ramp seed to germinate, and another two years for that seed to grow into a small bulb that sprouts two broad, smooth leaves about 6 to 8 inches in length and 2 to 3 inches across. A sizable, mature bulb should be at least 3 years old or more. In midsummer, the plant sends up a flower stalk with a white flower cluster which then bears small, round 1/8 inch seeds.

Where and When to Gather

Regionally, wild leeks are distributed as far east as New York State and through Canada, west into the forests of Wisconsin and Minnesota, and south into Appalachia. Wild leeks are plentiful in the well-drained soil of beech and maple hardwood forests along rivers and on the back dunes along the Great Lakes shoreline. The broad leaves of the wild leek are frequently found alongside unfolding mayapples and trout lily.

It takes about four (and up to six) years for a seed to develop into a mature, sizable leek (about 1 1/2 inch across) ready for harvesting. The bulbs can be easily dug with a garden fork, but only harvest the full plant in moderation. The most sustainable way to enjoy the wild leek is to only clip the tops for use in cooking.

How to Eat

The entire wild leek is edible, but in consideration of overharvesting, just clip the green tops to use in salads, soups, and seasonings. Cultivate your own wild stands to enjoy a small harvest of the bulb each year. The bulb is delicious pickled as a cocktail onion for martinis. It sweetens nicely when roasted and drizzled in olive oil. Or it can simply be chopped and added to a spring egg and nettle quiche or a foraged garlic mustard pesto pizza with morels. The tops can be used as a wild onion garnish in salads and to garnish and season cooked dishes.

Future Harvests

While they may seem to carpet the floor of the woods in the spring, there is growing concern for overharvesting wild leeks for the restaurant market and by hobby foragers. Take time to first learn the distribution of leeks in the area before harvesting, and choose to harvest tops only. Transplanting wild bulbs within the wild can help expand stands of the plant. Also, local growers are beginning to propagate wild leeks for private forest gardens, making this a sustainable option for the forager wishing to enjoy the bulbs in early spring.

wild lettuce

Lactuca species

EDIBLE leaves

The green leaves of wild lettuce are valuable to the forager in spring as raw early salad greens and then in the summer as cooked greens in stir-fries, frittatas, and soups.

Wild lettuce with a spiny midrib.

How to Identify

Wild lettuce is an annual or biennial plant that grows in a basal rosette, its leaves waxy and pinnately lobed. The stem is hairless, and the leaves grow large and continue alternately up the stem across the summer season. The mature leaves feature a notable spiny midrib (the spines disappear when the plant is cooked). Wild lettuce grows very tall when it bolts and goes to seed, up to 8 feet in height. The blooms are aster-like and yellow; they go to seed in small, fluffy seed heads. The leaves, stem, and flowers exude a brown-white, latex-like sap.

Where and When to Gather

Wild lettuce grows abundantly in disturbed waste places, open fields, and parking lots—it is not a high-maintenance garden flower. The tender spring leaves are best raw, and summer leaves are good for cooking.

How to Gather

While wild lettuce may grow with abandon nearly everywhere, harvest it only in low-traffic areas free of soil contamination and pollution. The early tender greens can be picked by hand and washed. The summer greens can also be picked off the stems by hand, washed, and then prepared for cooking in the kitchen. The spine will dissipate when cooked, as it is tender, not firm like a thorn. The entire basal rosette can be gathered before the plant goes to flower and then blanched and frozen for later use.

How to Eat

Use the early spring greens raw in salads. Toss them with other early spring greens like dandelion, dock, watercress, and garlic mustard. The ratio of bitter greens can also be offset with greens that are more neutral in flavor like violet leaves, trout lily, spring beauty, redbud leaves, or early leaves of the basswood or linden.

These foraged salad green mixes can be dressed with a simple mustard vinaigrette, which will help pull together the flavors of the greens and make them more palatable to those who are newcomers to foraged foods. Ginger or soy dressings also work well with these salads; top the mélange with foraged nuts and local cheeses. The goal of the forager is to learn the subtlety of each plant and how to balance the flavors so they are fully enjoyed at the table. Wild lettuce leaves become large and less tender as the summer unfolds, but they can still be used as cooked greens in stir-fries, frittatas, and soups.

Future Harvest

Wild lettuce propagates prolifically with its abundant release of seeds. Gathering its leaves across the season will do little to impact its distribution or future harvest.

wild onion

Allium canadense

EDIBLE bulb, leaves, flowers

A harbinger of warmer weather and relative of the wild garlic and wild leek, the early spring wild onion is easy to spot. Its pungent flavor also makes it very versatile in the forager's kitchen.

How to Identify

Wild onion is a clumping, perennial bulb, distinguished from field garlic (*Allium vineale*) and wild leek (*Allium tricoccum*) primarily by its elongated leaves. The leaves are narrow but flat, soft, and flaccid, not round, hollow, and wiry like those of field garlic. The bulblet is about the size of a pearl onion (smaller than the wild leek), and its domed flowerhead is full of whitish-pink blossoms. The wild onion dies back in the late spring or early summer. The entire plant is edible and smells of onion.

Wild onion in bloom.

Where and When to Gather

Wild onion pushes through the soil as soon as the snow melts away and the ground begins to thaw. It grows along trails and in fields in soil of relatively poor quality.

How to Gather

The entire plant can be dug and used in the kitchen, but clipping only the leaves helps ensure the wild onion's sustainability for future harvests. If using the whole plant, wash it well in the kitchen.

How to Eat

A favorite flavor of spring, wild onion is more pungent and aromatic than a culinary green onion and less garlicky than the wild garlic. Used raw, wild onion leaves are delicious cut into wild greens or an herbed spring salad. You can use wild onions in place of the common green onion in any recipe. Like field garlic, the bulb and rootlets can be chopped and included in cooked dishes, but they can be fibrous if not pureed or cooked down to make them more tender. The bulb, trimmed of the small rootlets, can be pickled and enjoyed in cocktails.

Future Harvests

The entire wild onion plant can be harvested. However, take care to remember that it is a bulb, so if you remove the bulb, you are removing the entire plant from the soil. Clip and use only the tops for the most sustainable harvesting.

wild peach

Prunus persica

EDIBLE fruit

A juicy wild peach is a delicious treat to discover in the height of summer. Gather and take it back to the kitchen to prepare in the many ways peaches shine, particularly as pie and jam.

How to Identify

Wild peach is a small fruit tree, growing to up to 25 feet high. The young wild peach has smooth gray bark with lenticels; the bark on older trees is cracked and rough.

The finely serrated, lance-shaped leaves grow alternately along the stems. In early spring, the wild peach tree is covered with pinkish five-petal flowers, and its small fruit ripens by early July.

Wild peaches ripening in the summer sun.

Where and When to Gather

Wild peaches can be found on the sunny
edges of the woodland and along trails.
Many wild peach trees have escaped
from gardens or are the remnants of old
orchards. The fruit ripens in early July.

How to Gather

Gather fruit that is soft to the touch, with
inner flesh that is soft and juicy, not hard
and green. Avoid insect-damaged fruit.
Peaches have a limited shelf life and should
be eaten fresh, prepared into preserves, or
sliced and frozen for later use.

How to Eat

While this foraged stone fruit may be
smaller than its cultivated counterpart, the
wild peach is just as delicious in jams and
pies. Puree the fruit for fruit leather or use
the puree in muffins or breads. Slice fresh
peaches and dry in a dehydrator for peach
snacks. Wild peaches can be served fresh
on cheese platters, added to sandwiches,
and tossed into fruit salads with other wild
fruits and berries.

Future Harvests

The wild peach is not an endangered
plant and is often found abandoned on
old homesteads with fruit left on the tree,
neglected. The forager should take delight
in gathering this fruit, which often is left
unharvested.

wild pear

Pyrus pyraster

`EDIBLE` fruit

Wild pears are similar in flavor but slightly smaller and a bit more firm than their cultivated Bartlett counterparts. From jams to compotes, to crumbles to strudels, wild pears can be a treasure in the kitchen.

Wild pears along a trail.

How to Identify

Wild pear is a small fruiting tree with gray bark that grows to heights of up to 20 feet. It produces a white five-petal blossom that gives way to fruit that ripens in late summer into early fall. The wild pear is smaller, more firm, and more spherical than the store-bought fruit.

Where and When to Gather

Look for wild pear along trails through old orchards and homesteads and along the edges of succession forests in full sun.

How to Gather

Choose pears that have fallen from the tree or detach easily from the branches. Take care to avoid fruit with significant insect damage. Fruit can be stored in a brown paper bag in the refrigerator for up to two weeks before processing or eating fresh, or it can be sliced and frozen for later use.

How to Eat

Enjoy wild pears fresh in savory salads, pairing them with bitter greens like chicory, arugula, or endive. Puree the fruit and use it as a fruit base for glazes and barbecue sauces. Throw fresh wild pears into a smoothie or poach them in red wine, then serve with a local cheese and foraged nuts.

Bake wild pears into strudels, muffins, pies, and crumbles, or stir them into a rice pudding. The pears can also be simmered with parsnips, groundnuts, sunchoke, or sweet potatoes, and then mashed and topped with foraged onion and field garlic. Wild pears can also be enjoyed sliced and dried in the dehydrator for an easy and simple fruit snack.

Future Harvests

The fruit of the wild pear is frequently neglected and should be gathered and enjoyed. Harvesting the fruit will do little to affect this plant's abundance and sustainability. The wild pear can easily be integrated into any permaculture or food forest plan to add edible plantings back into our landscape.

wild plum

Prunus americana
American plum

`EDIBLE` fruit

In rustic tarts and barbecue sauces, the native wild plum shines. Its small wild fruits can be transformed into so many delicious sweet and savory dishes in the kitchen.

How to Identify

Wild plum is a large, shrub-like fruiting tree with a rough, spiny, and gray bark. Its leaves are smooth, ovate, alternate, and green. It blooms in late spring with an aromatic, white, five-petal flower that blossoms singly or in clusters. The fruit is smaller than domesticated cultivars; it ripens in late summer. The fruit ranges in color from red to blue-brown, and it has a yellowish dark flesh.

Where and When to Gather

Wild plum prefers edges of woodlands and succession forests, prairies, and open fields. Sometimes you can find it integrated

Wild plums ripening, ready to be gathered soon.

into municipal landscaping. In the spring, the trees are identifiable by the dusty, aromatic blossom. Look for the ripe fruit in late summer into October.

How to Gather

Choose ripe plums that are soft to the touch. Harvest on dry, warm summer days, as the warmth of the sun helps sweeten the sugars in the fruit. Harvesting on wet, rainy days will result in a more fragile and less sweet fruit. Process immediately in the kitchen as ripe fruit has a very short shelf life and can mold easily.

How to Eat

The sweet, soft flesh of the wild plum can be enjoyed straight off the tree as a juicy foraging snack. In the kitchen, only the cook's imagination can limit the use of the wild plum. It can be preserved like any other summer fruit—puree it for fruit leathers, or make it into jams, compotes, or pastry filling. Of course, you could always make wild plum crumbles, wild plum tarts, and wild plum cakes.

Consider featuring this stone fruit as the centerpiece of a meal, sliced raw over fresh local cheeses and drizzled in honey. Dried slices of wild plum can be wrapped in prosciutto, skewered, and grilled or broiled to make a savory appetizer. The wild plum can be a versatile base for a rich barbecue sauce, as it works well with sweet tomato, ancho, or soy-based flavors. For dessert, wild plums can be poached in red wine or glazed with honey and broiled. Serve this treat with fresh yogurt, or homemade ice cream.

Future Harvests

While a native species, the wild plum is also a feral cultivar. Gathering the ignored fruit will do little to harm the plant's future sustainability. As a fruiting tree, American plum is a nice addition to a permaculture garden.

wild rice

Zizania species

EDIBLE grains

While not a rice at all, this native grass of the upper Midwest has historically provided local people with a staple carbohydrate that is rich in proteins and minerals, as well as a true taste of the terroir.

Wild rice in flower along the banks of a river.

Finishing the wild rice kernels over an open fire, to dry the chaff.

How to Identify

Wild rice grows in shallow waters, loosely rooted to the submerged soil. In late spring, the annual grass grows tall from its matted spread on the water. Its stalk is thick and hollow, with long, slender leaves, and can range in height from 3 feet to over 10 feet. In early summer, it grows a delicate and wispy panicle (seed plume) 1 to 2 feet in length. The panicle has female parts above and drooping male plant parts below. The seed kernels are produced in late summer; they release easily from the panicle, are soft and "milky" (like milky oats), and vary in color from yellow to green to light purplish.

Where and When to Gather

Wild rice grows in the cold shallow waters of the upper Midwest, loosely rooted to the soils in running waters in marshland. It rarely grows in stagnant water. The kernels of rice ripen at different times, beginning in late summer. Harvesting season runs only a few short weeks.

How to Gather

A canoe makes gathering the kernels of rice an easy task as it allows one to float along the banks, tapping the kernels of ripened rice (which is soft and green) with ricing sticks (or simply two whittled-down sapling sticks made into paddles). The ripe kernels will fall easily into your boat, the bottom of which should be covered with a clean tarp to gather your harvest and prevent dirt and sand from getting into the grains.

The harvested kernels will be filled with moisture and need to be dried and then cured to prevent mold from growing and ruining the seed. This process is called finishing and drying. Depending on the quantity, the kernels can be laid in the sun on the tarp, turned frequently, and dried over the course of a few days.

The kernels should then be dry-finished in a pan and over a heat source (in a pot over a fire, iron skillet over the stove, or in the oven on a cookie sheet) to dry the hull and allow it to be easily winnowed. Don't burn, scorch, or even toast the rice. Parching it for a few minutes is sufficient to dry the chaff. Then the chaff can be separated from the kernel and the kernels stored for later use. It is important to separate the kernel from the chaff immediately after parching so the kernel doesn't rehydrate, so plan that into the processing time. To winnow small batches of rice (remove the chaff and other materials), simply rub the kernels between your hands. When it is winnowed, spread it out into a thin layer on a baking sheet on top of a table and meticulously sort through it with tweezers, removing worms and broken pieces of stalks.

How to Eat

Enjoy the flavors of wild rice at any mealtime—for breakfast with maple syrup and foraged walnuts, or at dinner in side dishes that complement your foraged vegetables or hunted game. As with any grain, it is useful to soak the rice kernels overnight before cooking, as this helps improve digestibility. The general cooking time for wild rice is similar to cultivated rice grains. Use a 1:2.5 ratio of rice to water. Simmer on the stove for 35 minutes, or cook it in a rice or pressure cooker. Adding a homemade bone broth or nettle broth when you cook the grain adds nutrition and flavor. Use cooked rice in rice salads and rice puddings. It is especially nice with holiday meals.

Future Harvests

While wild rice is a hearty annual plant, many things threaten it, including habitat loss and the loss of knowledge on how to harvest of wild rice. Much of today's "wild rice" isn't wild at all, but rather a crop that is now intensively cultivated with timed harvesting practices that negate the effects of weather, blight, and other factors. Working with native peoples to preserve their rights to cultivate and promote their tradition of the truly wild rice and its harvesting will help the preserve the plant. Consider following the traditional community's practice of gratitude while harvesting wild rice, offering thanks for both the food and spirit that continues on in this important plant.

wild sarsaparilla

Aralia nudicaulis

EDIBLE root

Sarsaparilla has a spicy, aromatic root that tastes similar to fruit-flavored cereal. It has a sweetness on the palate and can flavor not only homemade root beer but also teas and other cocktail beverages as well.

How to Identify

Wild sarsaparilla is a small, low-growing woodland plant standing about 18 inches tall. Its stem is woody, and the plants spread by runners. The plant typically has one very large lead at the top of the hairless stem, and that lead is divided into three parts with five leaflets each. The flowers are 1-inch white clusters on a main stem. The roots are slender, whitish, and aromatic.

A small stand of wild sarsaparilla along the edge of a trail in the woods.

Where and When to Gather

Sarsaparilla is a woodland plant that prefers moist soil in maple hardwood forests across the Midwest. The aromatic roots and runners can be gathered in early spring or late fall.

How to Gather

In areas with only a few plants, take care to harvest only the runners between the individual plants. Because tea requires a good deal of plant material, also consider making a plant extract with alcohol or glycerin instead of drying the roots so as not to overharvest an existing stand.

How to Eat

The roots and runners can be made into a simple syrup to flavor homemade sodas, like traditional root beer. Spicebush berries, wild ginger, and burdock root are all foraged plants that can work well with the flavors of sarsaparilla in a homemade soda or pair with a spicy rum for a forager's cocktail. Make a spicy and aromatic bitters blend with the roots, aspen bark, tulip poplar tips and branches, and a tad of molasses for sweetness. Herbalists also use the leaves, berries, and root in teas that some say can help people better withstand stress.

Future Harvests

Harvesting the entire rootstock of the sarsaparilla can negatively impact the plant, of course. Depending on the local range and availability of the plant, consider gathering the midsections or runners of the rootstock between the plants, without disturbing the attached individual plants. Sarsaparilla can be propagated by root cuttings in well-drained, rich, loamy woodland soil.

wild strawberry

Fragaria species

EDIBLE berries

The entirety of summer can be tasted in one bite of a petite wild strawberry. More intense in flavor than its cultivated counterpart and significantly smaller, the wild strawberry is tedious to collect, but oh so rewarding.

Small wild strawberry blossoms in late springtime.

How to Identify

Wild strawberry is a low-growing, herbaceous plant with toothed, three-part leaflets at the end of a hairy, slender stem. The white flower clusters begin to bloom in late spring and give way to small, red strawberry fruit in early summer. The leaves remain on the plant through the fall and turn a deep red color in autumn, helpful for off-season identification.

Where and When to Gather

Wild strawberry can be found in open fields and meadows; moist, well-drained soils of hedgerows; and along the edges of the wood, oftentimes in tall grasses. The berries ripen about the same time as summer solstice. Finding a patch large enough for a big harvest can be tough, but it's worth the effort of seeking out (and then certainly keeping a secret).

How to Gather

Gather the small berries into berry baskets or trays, taking care not to crush the delicate fruit. Avoid gathering berries that are dirty or moldy. Berries can be processed immediately or frozen whole (with the green tops removed) for later use.

How to Eat

Enjoy wild strawberries right off the bush under the high summer sun. They are much more intensely flavored than the cultivated berry, so jams, pies, or any baked good will taste delicious. Puree the fruits through a food mill to remove the green leaf calyx and extra seeds. Use the puree in fruit leather and for a berry sauce. A good harvest warrants a round of fresh wild strawberry daiquiris. And, of course, there's always strawberry shortcake made with homemade angel food cake and topped with fresh whipped cream.

Future Harvests

Wild strawberries are fairly common and propagate easily with runners, so gathering the fruit will do little to affect future harvests of the plant. Of more concern is habitat loss. To increase the stands of the wild strawberry, you could easily incorporate this plant into the woodland or open field areas of a permaculture landscape plan.

wintergreen

Gaultheria procumbens

EDIBLE berries, leaves

Most popularly known as the flavor of teaberry gum, wintergreen is a common woodland plant. You can collect its leaves and berries for baking, desserts, cocktails, tea, and herbal remedies.

Wintergreen with berries in the summer.

How to Identify

Wintergreen is a small, herbaceous, evergreen perennial plant that grows up to 6 inches in the shade of the forest. Its small leaves are ovate and oblong, dark and shiny green (they turn reddish in winter). Wintergreen has small, white, bell-shaped flowers that dangle below the leaves and bloom in early spring. The flowers give way to delicious small red berries in late May and early June. The leaves are aromatic of wintergreen when crushed, while the berries have a bright fruity smell.

Where and When to Gather

Wintergreen grows in maple hardwood forests in sandy, well-drained soil. The plant spreads by runners, and it will eventually blanket an entire small area. The leaves can be gathered any time across the year, but they seem to be more aromatic in spring. The berries have a small window for harvesting: look for them at the end of May into early June.

How to Gather

Since each plant is fairly small, pick only one leaf from each plant so as not to strip it of its ability to photosynthesize. The leaves can be used fresh or dried on a screen or in a dehydrator for later use. The berries can be picked by hand and used fresh or dried for later use (though I never get home with many in my basket as I eat them along the way).

How to Eat

The flavor of wintergreen is very useful in the kitchen. The leaves can be made into a simple syrup that can be used as a flavoring agent in desserts, such as ice cream, chocolate truffles, chocolate flourless cake, or mousse. Consider making hard candies and mints with the syrup.

A wintergreen simple syrup can also be used to make cocktails, and the leaves can be directly infused into vodkas and spicy rums and sweetened with honey for an infused wintergreen cordial. The aromatic wintergreen is also delicious as a layer in a cocktail bitters mix, and it mixes well with tulip poplar, blackberry, coffee, and dark rum flavors.

As an herbal remedy, wintergreen tea has been used across time to soothe an upset stomach. Infuse wintergreen leaves in olive oil to make into a topical salve with beeswax for a relaxing and good-smelling muscle balm.

Wintergreen berries have a light, fruity taste with a wintergreen fresh flavor. They can be dried for snacking, baking, or used fresh in ice creams or desserts—if any make it home from your foraging jaunt.

Future Harvests

Wintergreen is a delightfully small plant, so harvest the leaves considering its size to ensure enough leaves and berries remain and the plant can continue to flourish in the future.

wood sorrel

Oxalis species

`EDIBLE` leaves

The tiny, tender spring greens of wood sorrel taste bright and citrusy. They can be gathered by the handful for use in salads and soups or as a flavorful garnish for sandwiches and main dishes.

How to Identify

Wood sorrel grows from a tiny perennial bulb. Like clover, it has three leaflets per leaf. Unlike clover, each of the leaflets is heart-shaped. The thin, fragile-looking leaflets have the unusual ability to fold in half at night, during a rainstorm, or when the soil is too dry for the plant's liking. The three-part leaflets are attached by a smooth and succulent stem. Sorrel flowers have five petals and can vary in color from yellow to whitish pink. The leaves taste markedly tart and citrusy.

Tiny wood sorrel can be gathered beginning in mid-spring and throughout the summer. The thin, fragile-looking leaflets have the unusual ability to fold in half at night, during a rainstorm, or when the soil is too dry.

Where and When to Gather

Wood sorrel enjoys partial to full shade and can be found at the edges of the trail, in open fields and woodlands, and near the base of trees. It's a common plant and is easily found from spring until fall.

How to Gather

Gather the leaves by hand. While the bulb is edible, cut only the tops, and the plant will yield successive harvests. Wood sorrel doesn't have a long shelf life, so plan to eat it soon after picking.

How to Eat

This is a versatile green, not overly bitter or astringent. Kids have fun gathering wood sorrel because they enjoy the adventure of looking for "lucky shamrocks." It has a pleasant flavor that pairs well with most other greens.

Incorporate wood sorrel greens into a salad of violet and dandelion leaves, or top a watercress salad with sorrel leaves and blossoms. Garnish sandwiches with the tangy greens, wrap them up in a pita sandwich, or use them on a BLT in place of the lettuce. It's a nice addition to a radish and butter sandwich, too. Wood sorrel can also be added to a pesto for a tangy, citrus flavor.

Future Harvests

Wood sorrel is a common plant. If you gather only the top leaves, there will be greens to enjoy throughout the season.

wormwood

Artemisia species

artemisia

EDIBLE leaves

Mixologists and bartenders know wormwood (or artemisia) as the classic, primary herb in absinthe. It is a powerful addition to your foraged cocktail cart and bar.

Wormwood is strongly bitter and aromatic, a classic cocktail herb for the home bartender.

Wormwood tolerates poor quality soils and rocky outcrops. It is considered invasive in some parts.

How to Identify

Wormwood is an herbaceous perennial that grows to an average height of 4 feet. Its smooth, silvery, and pinnately lobed leaves are 2 to 3 inches long and grow up the stem of the plant. The flowers are clustered yellow heads that grow from the axils of the leaves.

Where and When to Gather

Wormwood loves hot, dry soil in the full sun; it tolerates rocky, craggy outcrops and disturbed areas. New growth in early spring is more aromatic than bitter, especially before flowering.

How to Gather

Gather wormwood leaves in spring before it begins to flower for the most aromatics. The leaves can be used fresh or dried and stored in an airtight container for later use.

How to Eat

Many cocktail recipes feature wormwood. It's a chief flavor in vermouth, absinthe, and classic cocktails like the Sazerac. The leaves can be infused directly into vodka to make a plant extract for flavoring cocktails or to make into an elixir by sweetening it with honey. Wormwood-infused vodka can be the base for a simple cocktail bitters—good on its own or blended with other flavors including citrus and dark rums. Artemisia can also be used to spice honey meads or homemade walnut nocino liqueur. As an herbal apothecary staple, the bitters of artemisia are a must for settling an upset stomach.

Future Harvests

Wormwood is a wild-growing, perennial herb. Gathering its new growth will not affect the plant and can help encourage the growth of new shoots.

yarrow

Achillea millefolium

EDIBLE flowers, leaves

Yarrow is a beautiful, perennial wildflower that dots fields and open spaces in the summertime landscape. Its aromatic, bitter flavor makes it a useful herb for brewing beer, making cocktail bitters, and flavoring beverages.

How to Identify

Yarrow grows to be 2 to 3 feet in height, with tall erect stems that have flat, umbel-like flowers made up of many five-petaled blooms that range in color from white to pinkish white and even purple. The leaves appear fine and hairy, but actually they are lance-shaped and cut into many small, silvery gray segments, growing in a basal rosette and then alternating up the stem. The finely divided appearance of the leaves is an aid

Yarrow is a perennial herb that grows alone or in large stands like this one.

Yarrow blooms in early to midsummer. The flowers are aromatic and markedly bitter.

to identification and is how yarrow got its species name, *millefolium*, or thousand leaves.

Cultivars of yarrow that are deep yellow have found favor for use in floral arrangements and ornamental landscaping. They are more resinous, but sometimes escape gardens and end up wild. These can be used similarly to the white yarrow found in the wild.

Where and When to Gather

A hardy perennial and native wildflower that prefers full sun, yarrow can often be found in open fields. It blooms toward the beginning of the summer solstice and continues to bloom through the end of July. The flavors and mild aromatics of the flowers can remain through the fall; however, I always suggest you go by your nose to test for yarrow's strength in the off-season.

How to Gather

Yarrow is a perennial herb. Depending on the size of the stand, the entire stalk can be gathered. Take care, however, not to cut down the entire plant. Stalks can be bundled toward their bottom ends and hung to dry for later use.

Yarrow's finely toothed leaves are a chief botanical signature of the plant. The leaves taste aromatic and bitter like the flowers.

How to Use

Yarrow is aromatic: its flavors are predominantly bitter with a hint of warming spice. The plant is also astringent, leaving your tongue dry when you taste the leaves or drink yarrow tea. As it is bitter, mixologists can use it to create a brightly flavored cocktail bitter. Yarrow has been known to brewers for many years as a classic bitter brewing herb, and the lore around using yarrow in brewing is abundant. Yarrow's warming spicy notes and predominantly bitter flavor profile can work well in IPA-style recipes. Take care, though, to monitor yarrow's tendency to be overly bitter. This can be managed by adding yarrow to the second fermentation of a brew process: the longer it processes, the more prominent the bitter flavor and less aromatic it will be.

Future Harvest

Yarrow is a perennial native wildflower. If care is given to only harvest just basal leaves or a stalk or two from each plant, it will regrow for you each year.

yellow birch

Betula alleghaniensis

EDIBLE tips of branches, leaves, sap

The taste of wintergreen flavors your mouth as you chew the tender tips of the young branches of the yellow birch tree. Its sap can be collected in spring to produce a savory syrup delicious in recipes, baking, and beverage making.

How to Identify

Of the various *Betula* species, yellow birch is most abundant across the Midwest. It is a fast-growing hardwood, commonly found in rich, well-drained soils, particularly near streams and rivers. It is also commonly used in ornamental landscaping

The bark is a smooth, dark gray-black, scored horizontally with lenticels. The leaves are alternate and serrated, and

The leaves of the yellow birch.

The catkins of the yellow birch in fall.

The bark of the yellow birch.

male catkins form in late winter before the leaves break open from their resinous buds. An accurate way to identify the tree is the distinct smell and flavor of wintergreen from tender new branches or leaves. If there is a notable almond-forward note or flavor in the branches, then you have most likely discovered a cherry tree (*Prunus* species). The yellow birch is also host for the popular chaga mushroom, a delicious fungus that has a variety of culinary and medicinal properties.

Where and When to Gather

Gather the small twigs and branches in the early spring when the sap is flowing and the flavors of wintergreen are most prominent. (See aspen for more about collecting and processing bark.) Connect with area "sugar bushers" if you have questions about the timing of the sap run as the birch sap collection time is a bit later than the maple syrup time.

How to Gather

Using pruning shears or clippers, snip off the tender spring growth of the branches, leaf buds, and leaves, then dry for tea. Store in an airtight container to preserve the wintergreen flavor and nose, as the volatile oils are prone to evaporation.

To collect the sap, seek out stands and select trees that are at least 6 to 8 inches in diameter for tapping. An abundance of yellow birch sap is needed to be boiled down into a usable syrup—about 60 gallons boiled down will produce about 1 gallon of yellow birch syrup. (To learn how to gather sap and convert it to syrup, see maple.)

How to Eat

The wintergreen flavor of the tender, fresh twigs and leaves can be infused into a gentle and relaxing tea. Combine yellow birch with sassafras, spicebush, burdock, and sarsaparilla for a warming and locally flavored chai tea.

The yellow birch in the fall.

The sap can be boiled down outside (do not attempt to make syrup indoors) to make a savory syrup. The flavor is similar to molasses rather than maple syrup, with an ever-so-slight backnote of wintergreen—though note the wintergreen won't be prominent as the majority of any of the birch's aromatics will be boiled off in the sap-making process. The sap can be fermented with foraged herbs like spicebush or sassafras root or culinary herbs such as clove or orange peel and honey into a sweetened beverage that today is known as birch beer.

Future Harvests

The yellow birch is a fast-growing tree, abundant across the Midwest. Tapping mature trees and harvesting the tips of branches are both sustainable harvesting strategies that won't harm the tree when done in moderation.

Metric Conversions

Inches	Centimeters		Feet	Meters
1/4	0.6		1	0.3
1/3	0.8		2	0.6
1/2	1.3		3	0.9
3/4	1.9		4	1.2
1	2.5		5	1.5
2	5.1		6	1.8
3	7.6		7	2.1
4	10		8	2.4
5	13		9	2.7
6	15		10	3
7	18			
8	20			
9	23			
10	25			

Temperatures

degrees Celsius = $\frac{5}{9} \times$ (degrees Fahrenheit − 32)

degrees Fahrenheit = ($\frac{9}{5} \times$ degrees Celsius) + 32

To convert length:	Multiply by:
Yards to meters	0.9
Inches to centimeters	2.54
Inches to millimeters	25.4
Feet to centimeters	30.5

Suggested Further Reading

Much of my learning has come from direct, hands-on experience, and I cannot emphasize enough how much you can learn just by spending time with the plants in the field and in the kitchen. In addition to hands-on experience, I encourage you to slowly grow your own plant library that should include field guides, recipe books, and nature writings. Here are a few books from my wild foods library that I think you may find useful on your own learning journey:

A Sampling of Recommended Wild Foods Reading

Brill, Steve. *Identifying and Harvesting Edible and Medicinal Plants in Wild (and Not So Wild) Places.* New York, NY: HarperCollins, 1994.

Cook, Langdon. *Fat of the Land.* Seattle, WA: Skipstone, 2009.

Elpel, Thomas. *Botany in a Day: The Patterns Method of Plant Identification.* Pony, MT: HOPS Press, 1996.

Gibbons, Euell. *Stalking the Wild Asparagus.* New York, NY: D. McKay Co., 1962.

Learner, Rebecca. *Dandelion Hunter: Foraging the Urban Wilderness.* Guilford, CT: Lyons Press, 2013.

Rinella, Steve. *The Scavenger's Guide to Haute Cuisine.* New York, NY: Hyperion, 2005.

Shaw, Hank. *Hunt, Gather, Cook: Finding the Forgotten Feast.* New York, NY: Rodale, 2011.

Thayer, Samuel. *Nature's Garden: A Guide to Identifying, Harvesting, and Preparing Wild Edible Plants.* Birchwood, WI: Forager's Harvest, 2010.

Thayer, Samuel. *The Forager's Harvest: A Guide to Identifying, Harvesting and Preparing Edible Wild Plants.* Ogema, WI: Forager's Harvest, 2006.

Voss, Edward. *Field Manual of Michigan Flora.* Ann Arbor, MI: University of Michigan Press, 2012.

Online Resources

There is a growing web presence of online foraging-specific expertise. Here are just a few of my colleagues' sites:

Butter Wilde: *hungerandthirstforlife. blogspot.com/*

Hank Shaw: honest-food.net/author/hank/

Leda Meredith: ledameredith.net/ wordpress/

Rebecca Lerner: *firstways.com*

Rebecca McTrouble: cauldronsandcrockpots.com/

Steve Brill: wildmanstevebrill.com/

Wild Food Girl, Forager: wildfoodgirl.com/

Acknowledgments

The production of a book is no small feat. To all my friends and dear family who both supported me and have tolerated me throughout the production process, thank you. I appreciate your love and support.

A big shout out goes to my team at Timber Press whose enthusiasm for the project and helpfulness in curating a final product has been foundational in getting this book to market. As part of my extended production team, I cannot fail to mention the gratitude I have for Holly Bechiri and Mike Krebill. Holly has now helped me survive the production of two books, and she continues to cheer me on as I embark upon writing a third. Holly never holds back her comments, and I believe the end product is always better for it. And Mike's years of wild foods experience and many hours dedicated to the review of this book have also helped me a great deal. Mike also kept me amused by including his own foraging stories in the margins of my revisions. For his humor and knowledge, I am grateful. I am also glad for the growing friendships with fellow foragers across the country including (but of course not limited to) Leda Meredith, Hank Shaw, Butter Wilde, and Sam Thayer.

Above all, I must thank my Dad for teaching me to listen to the earth, to watch the wind, soil, sun, and clouds and learn from them. He was the first naturalist in my life and to him this book is dedicated.

Photo Credits

Special thanks go to my forager friends and to other generous photographers who offered use of their photos for the production of this book:

Chris Bennett, page 202
Cindee Dresden, page 288
Troy Evans, Great Smoky Mountains
    National Park, Bugwood.org, page 191
Wendy VanDyk Evans, page 39
Mike Krebill, pages 42, 43, 51, 52, 65, 136,
    151, 160, 285

Leda Meredith, pages 37, 126, 168, 198, 281
Rob Routledge, Sault College, Bugwood.org,
    page 192
Walter Siegmund, page 250
Seth Starner, pages 9, 113
Sam Thayer, pages 39, 133, 147, 247, 287
Angelyn Whitmeyer, pages 72, 99, 303, 304

All other photos are by the author.

Index

About the Author

JONATHON STONER

Lisa M. Rose is an herbalist, forager, urban farmer, and writer. With a background in anthropology and a professional focus on community health, she has gathered her food, farming, and wild plant knowledge from many people and places along a very delicious journey.

Beyond the Great Lakes, Lisa's interest in ethnobotany and herbal medicine has taken her across the United States and into the Yucatan, mainland Mexico, Nicaragua, and Brazil to study plants, people, health, and their connection to place.

When she is not in her own gardens or kitchen, Lisa can be found in the fields and forests, leading foraging plant walks and teaching classes on edible and medicinal wild plants. She forages for her own family, herbal apothecary, and community herbalism practice with her favorite harvesting companion—her dog, Rosie.